Crime Scene
Investigators

TEN TRUE TALES

Crime Scene Investigators

Allan Zullo

SCHOLASTIC INC.

New York Toronto London Auckland Sydney
Mexico City New Delhi Hong Kong Buenos Aires

ISBN-13: 978-0-439-93406-0
ISBN-10: 0-439-93406-0

Copyright © 2008 by The Wordsellers, Inc.

12 11 10 9 8 7 6 5 4 3 2   8 9 10 11 12 13/0

Printed in the U.S.A.
First Scholastic printing, January 2008

To my grandson Chad Manausa,
with hopes he will always question, always
probe, and always explore to satisfy his
curiosity and learn the truth. —A.Z.

Contents

Crime Scene Investigators

Perps and Vics

At virtually every crime scene, the criminal leaves behind some barely detectable clue of his or her presence and often unwittingly carries away something that is directly linked to the crime. It could be a drop of blood, a strand of hair, a fingerprint. Today, law-enforcement agencies are solving cases by finding and analyzing such trace evidence.

This process is known as forensics — using science and technology to investigate and establish facts in criminal cases. The people involved in forensics are part of a crime-scene investigation (CSI) team that includes detectives, technicians, medical examiners, scientists, and laboratory analysts.

This book features 10 gripping stories of detectives and CSI members who cracked difficult cases — from kidnapping to murder — by discovering trace evidence that connected the villain to the victim. You will read how seemingly insignificant things such as dirt under the fingernails, a scratch on the fender of a car, or balled-up paper in a wastebasket helped police capture cold-blooded killers.

Each story is written from the point of view of the lead detective and members of the CSI team as they collect clues that ultimately point to the criminal (sometimes referred to by police as the "perp," which is short for perpetrator). These stories are based on real cases taken from police files and court documents. Although the basic details of these cases are accurate (including their locations), the dialogue and many scenes have been dramatized, and the names have been changed to protect everyone's privacy. In some stories, two or more real-life investigators were combined into one character for dramatic purposes.

Solving crimes is not for the faint of heart, and neither is reading about them. This book is not for the squeamish, because some of the cases involve splattered blood, dead bodies, and charred bones.

The CSI team often must look past the gruesome sight of a dead victim (sometimes called a "vic" by police) as they search for the tiniest shreds of evidence in order to catch the perp. One of the most important clues the CSI team hopes to find is DNA (abbreviation for deoxyribonucleic acid). Found in the majority of the body's cells, DNA carries the genetic instructions that each person inherits from his or her parents. No two people have exactly the same DNA, except for identical twins. As a result, DNA can help identify a suspect or an unknown victim and is more accurate than fingerprints. Investigators have found DNA from the saliva left on a ski mask, toothpick, and cigar butt; and in the sweat left on a baseball cap, sneaker, and even a gold ring.

A CSI technician's microscope can be just as powerful a weapon as a police officer's gun in nabbing perps. For example, laboratory analysis can determine if someone else's hair found on the victim has been dyed, cut in a certain way, or pulled out. The hair can then be compared to the suspect's. Dirt, dust particles, pollen, and seeds on a suspect's clothing or body can sometimes reveal where he or she had been. Finding such clues on a murder victim can help determine whether the corpse had been moved. Analysis of fibers collected at the crime scene can often link the victim to a suspect's clothing, drapery, carpeting, blanket, or furniture.

Thanks to the skills and technology of CSI teams who are uncovering valuable trace evidence, more dangerous criminals than ever before are being captured and brought to justice. In the following pages are 10 such compelling cases.

— The —
Case of the
Three-time
Loser

The moment Detective Paula Hammond stepped into the sprawling home in the upscale neighborhood in suburban Columbia, South Carolina, she felt an immediate wave of sadness. The house, which had been adorned with expensive antiques in every room, looked like a mini-tornado had ripped through it. Dresser drawers had been yanked out, and the contents dumped helter-skelter. Exquisite ceramics and wood carvings — mementoes of travels to far-flung places — had been swept from their shelves and lay scattered and broken on the floor. Chairs and tables had been tossed on their sides or backs.

The mother of two teenage sons, the tall 40-year-old investigator looked as trim and fit as her college days playing basketball for Clemson. Her gentle manner and wholesome looks belied the fact that she was really a tough-as-nails homicide detective.

"Where's the body?" she asked Sergeant Steve Culpepper.

"In the basement. He was shot at least twice."

Down the hall, Hammond saw an elderly woman in a leather chair, her arms folded, rocking back and forth. The detective walked over to her, bent down, and gently clasped the woman's hand. "Mrs. Dietz, I'm deeply sorry for your loss. I can't begin to imagine the shock and grief you must be feeling right now."

"I'm too numb to cry and too hurt to move," moaned the 78-year-old woman. "Sixty years. We would have been married sixty years next month. Now I'll have to celebrate our anniversary at the cemetery."

"Mrs. Dietz, would you like to leave the house while the crime-scene investigators search for evidence? I can ask you questions later."

"No, Joseph would want me to be strong and stay here. Go about your business, Detective. I'll be right here to talk whenever you're ready."

Hammond squeezed the woman's hand and said, "We're pretty good at solving murders. Criminals usually leave some kind of evidence — even microscopic — that eventually leads us to them."

Culpepper took the detective downstairs, where the body of 81-year-old Joseph Dietz, a retired physician, lay on the floor in a pool of blood. The victim's head was covered by a towel.

"The killer threw the towel over the victim after he shot him, probably so the perp didn't have to see what he'd done," said Culpepper. "I think he gained entry by breaking the basement window and slipping inside. He ransacked the place looking for valuables, and at some point he murdered Dr. Dietz with a nine-millimeter Luger [a German pistol]."

Culpepper had found two spent cartridge casings on the bloody floor near the body. After placing two juice glasses over them to protect them while the CSI team worked the room, he measured their distance to the body.

Hammond went over to forensic pathologist Carter Newberry, who was still examining the body. "The victim shows signs that he put up a struggle," Newberry told her. "He was hit hard in the head and chest, but scrapes on his knuckles indicate he fought back." Pointing to the arms, he said, "See these bruises on his forearms? They're consistent with defensive movements. The downward angle of the bullet wounds tells me that he was falling back or was on his knees when he was shot from very close range. In fact, the gun was fired so close to him that it left a muzzle impression on his skin."

The detective noticed that the base of the victim's fourth finger on his left hand was not as tanned as the rest of his hand. "Looks like this killer was so heartless he stole the doctor's wedding ring," she said.

After taking out her small notebook, Hammond began making a sketch of the room, noting the location of the doors, broken window, and furniture. Meanwhile, the CSI photographer was shooting from all four corners of the room so the photos would show all perspectives of the crime scene for later viewing.

Using large brushes made of ostrich feathers and smaller ones made of soft bristles, two CSI members were dusting wood, metal, glass, plastic, and tile for fingerprints. Technician Kate Winthrop, who was examining the sill beneath the broken basement window, announced, "I've found a good set."

Most people's fingers carry a coating of perspiration and oil. When fingers come into contact with any relatively smooth surface, oil is released between the unique ridges and folds of the fingertips. When powder is applied to the surface, it sticks to the oil and brings out the pattern of the fingerprints.

Pulling a small brush out of her kit, Winthrop shook it until the bristles spread apart and became fluffy. She poured a little powder on a piece of paper and used it as a palette. Dipping the tip of the brush in the powder, she tapped gently to remove excess powder and brushed lightly in short, uniform strokes.

To lift the powdered print from the surface of the sill, she used a high-quality clear transparent tape. Rolling the tape a little at a time, she made sure not to get her own fingerprints on the tape. She pulled the roll so the rest of the exposed tape remained slightly taut, covering the entire fingerprint area. She was careful not to get air bubbles under the tape because they would destroy the value of the print. After gently rubbing the tape over the print, she slowly lifted off the print and placed the tape onto an evidence card.

"We're finding several sets of prints in other parts of the house," Winthrop told the detective. "We'll need to study them closer back at the lab, but the prints all look like they belong to the same person."

Hammond went outside to examine the backyard and soon spotted a half-smoked cigar in the grass. She called over Winthrop, who was carrying a kit that included special containers for holding various kinds of trace evidence. "The perp might have smoked this. If so, we should find his DNA on it," said the detective as she watched Winthrop carefully use tweezers to place the cigar in a plastic bag and seal it.

Hammond pointed to a brick lying in a bed of mulch next to the broken basement window. "Take that brick, too. The perp probably used it to break the window so he could reach in, unlock the latch, and open it."

"Hopefully he left his DNA from the sweat of his hand when he held the brick," said Winthrop.

Returning to the living room, the detective again offered condolences to the grieving widow and coaxed her to relive the last few hours.

"Joseph planned to read and take a nap, so I went shopping at the mall," Mrs. Dietz explained. "I returned about five o'clock, and the moment I entered the house, I knew something terrible had happened. Things were scattered all over the place."

She took a sip of water, needing two trembling hands to hold the glass. "I called out to Joseph, but there was no response. I hurried next door and asked my neighbor Marty Cohen to come back with me. He went through the house and couldn't find Joseph. The basement door was open, so he went down there, then ran back up and said that Joseph was dead" — her voice cracked — "that he had been shot in cold blood."

She began to weep. Hammond held the woman's hand and gently stroked it. "Do you know of anyone who wanted to harm your husband, Mrs. Dietz?"

"Everyone loved Joseph. He was active in the community and had scores of friends. All his patients loved him, and he loved them. He was making house calls at all hours of the day and night, long after other doctors in town quit doing it. It was hard for everyone when he finally retired three years ago. Friends and patients threw him a big thank-you party. What I'm trying to tell you, Detective, is that he had no enemies."

"My gut says this was a burglary that went horribly wrong, Mrs. Dietz. When you're up to it, I'll need a list and description of items that were taken. The burglar likely will be selling them to a fence [a person who knowingly buys stolen goods and then resells them]."

"Some of Joseph's guns are missing," said Mrs. Dietz. "He collected weapons of all kinds — fancy pistols, Civil War rifles, army guns, you name it."

Hammond couldn't help but think of the sad irony that shrouded the case. A man who had such an extensive gun collection was unable to defend himself against an intruder and wound up shot to death.

"Times sure have changed," said Mrs. Dietz. "No one is safe, not even in a nice neighborhood like this. And now I see all these female police people in my house. It's a whole new world."

Sergeant Culpepper came into the room and told the detective, "I interviewed a neighbor who might have encountered the perp. I think you should talk to him."

Hammond met with George Talbot, a retiree who lived three doors from the Dietzes. He told her, "About three-thirty, I was backing out of my driveway when a small silver car that had been parked in front of my house started driving off. I was halfway out into the street, and I slammed on my brakes. He banged into my rear bumper real hard and didn't even stop."

"Did you get a look at the driver?"

"He was a dark-skinned man in his late twenties and wearing a white hard hat. Everything happened so fast that I didn't get a license-plate number, darn it."

After seeing a nasty silver scratch on the bumper of Talbot's black car, Hammond called Winthrop over and asked her to scrape off the silver paint for analysis.

"Can you really determine the kind of car that hit mine just from the paint?" Talbot asked Winthrop.

"Many times," she replied. "There are more than forty thousand different types of auto paint classified in a database available to police. We often can get the year, make, and model of a car just from a few scrapings of paint."

Later that day, the crime lab confirmed the paint came from a silver Toyota Corolla that was four to six years old.

By now, the detective had an extensive list of the items taken during the burglary. Among them were six pistols; a diamond ring, earrings, necklaces, and bracelets worth more than $10,000; $250 in cash; gold coins worth $5,000; several silver pieces; and the victim's wedding band.

At police headquarters, Winthrop ran the fingerprints found at the Dietz house through a computer. Soon she had a match — Kermit Godby, a career criminal, who had been convicted and sentenced to prison twice. He completed a two-year sentence for armed robbery, and a year later was convicted again of another armed robbery for which he served half of a 15-year sentence before being released. He had been a free man for the past seven months.

Winthrop extracted DNA from both the cigar and brick found in the Dietzes' backyard. She compared it to a state database of DNA collected from every felon convicted in the state. (The FBI has a similar national database.) "The DNA samples at the murder scene absolutely, positively match Godby's," Winthrop told Hammond.

"How absolutely, positively?" the detective asked.

"Try two-point-six quadrillion — two-point-six followed by fifteen zeroes."

"He's definitely our man," said Hammond. "We've got to collar him."

Godby was supposedly living with his parents in Columbia. When Hammond and several officers arrived, they were met by Godby's mother. "I'm so worried about him," she told the detective. "I haven't seen hide nor hair of him in two days. Is he in trouble again?"

"Yes, Mrs. Godby, serious trouble," Hammond replied. "We need to question him as part of a murder investigation."

"Murder? Oh, lordy, my Kermit would never be involved in a murder. He's been straightening out his life ever since he got out of prison."

"Who does he hang out with?"

"Well, his best friend is Tank Snyder. He lives on the south end of town."

"What kind of car is Kermit driving?"

"He has my car — a 1999 silver Toyota Corolla."

After Mrs. Godby gave her the license number, the detective called dispatch to issue an all-points bulletin for the car.

Backed up by Culpepper and four officers, Hammond talked to Snyder, who admitted he saw Godby the previous day. "He showed me four guns — two Lugers and two Smith and Wessons — and asked me to get rid of them because they were hot [stolen]," Snyder said. "He shoved them in my hands and took off."

"What did you do with the guns?"

"I dumped them in a field a couple of blocks from here, because my mama doesn't want guns in the house."

Snyder led Hammond to an abandoned field where he had tossed the weapons. Police recovered three of them, including a Luger, which was taken immediately to the crime lab that would determine if it was the murder weapon.

Technicians can tell if a bullet comes from a specific gun. When a bullet travels through a gun barrel, the bullet's metal gets worn in a unique pattern by the harder metal of the barrel. Any bullet fired from a specific gun will show the same marks, so a CSI lab can positively identify the gun that the bullet came from.

Snyder told the detective that Godby was staying with B.J. Hendrix, who owned a body shop on Seventh and Broad streets. When Hammond, Culpepper, and the backup officers arrived there, she asked Hendrix where Godby was.

"He'll be back soon," he replied. "He went to get lunch for me and the boys."

"B.J., I need you to come clean," she said. "I know you've been busted before for fencing stolen goods. Tell me what Kermit gave you."

Hendrix put his hands halfway up and said, "He gave me two Glocks [an Austrian-manufactured handgun], and promised me they were clean [not stolen]."

"What did you do with them?"

"Sold them for eighty bucks apiece to a guy down the street."

She spotted the silver Corolla in the back, missing its front bumper. "What's up with the car, B.J.?"

"Kermit had a fender bender, and I offered to fix it."

"Out of the goodness of your heart?" she asked sarcastically. "What stolen goods did he give you in exchange for repairing the car?"

Hendrix sighed and motioned for her to follow him into the office. He opened a safe and pulled out a diamond ring that matched the description of the one stolen from the Dietzes' home. "Kermit said he won it in a poker game. I believed him. You're not going to bust me, are you?"

"It depends how things shake out today."

Hendrix pointed out the window. "There he is." Wearing a long-sleeved green shirt, jeans, and work boots, Godby was carrying a bag from a fast-food restaurant. He jaywalked across the street and stepped into the body shop's open garage.

With guns drawn, Hammond and the other police swooped down on Godby. "Get on the floor, spread your arms and legs, and stay that way!" she ordered. The officers pounced on him, pinned his arms behind his back, handcuffed him, and lifted him up.

"You're under arrest for burglary and murder," she told him.

"Murder? I didn't kill anyone," he claimed.

"You're lying, Kermit." Turning to Culpepper, she said, "Read him his rights."

The sergeant faced Godby and said, "You have the right to remain silent and refuse to answer questions. Anything you say may be used against you in a court of law. You have the right to consult an attorney before speaking to the police and to have an attorney present during questioning now or in the future. If you cannot afford an attorney, one will be appointed for you before any questioning if you wish. If you decide to answer questions now without an attorney present, you will still have the right to stop answering at any time until you talk to an attorney."

Later, in the police-interrogation room, Godby waived his right to an attorney and at first denied that he was ever in the Dietzes' house.

"Oh, spare me the lies, Kermit," scoffed Hammond. "We have your fingerprints all over the house. We have your DNA on a cigar in the backyard. We have a witness seeing you flee the area. And we have friends of yours who say you gave them guns and jewelry that we know were stolen from Dr. Dietz's home. Let's not play any more games, okay?"

Godby bowed his head and thought for a moment. "All right, you win. I broke into his house and stole the stuff. I admit it."

"And you shot Dr. Dietz."

"Shot him? No. No way. The truth is I found him dead when I broke in. You see, when I was in the joint [prison], I met a guy, Toby Brown. He had robbed Dietz a couple of years ago. Toby told me that when he got out, he was going to rob him again because the house was full of guns and jewelry. I didn't think anything more about it until I bumped into Toby the other day. He just got paroled. When I saw him, I remembered what he had said about Dietz, so I figured I better beat Toby to it or he'd steal it all.

"Last Monday afternoon, I drove to the neighborhood and parked my car a few doors away from Dietz's home. I carried a black duffel bag and wore a white hard hat and orange vest, so people would think I was a city worker. I knocked on the front door and no one answered, so I went around the back. I picked up a brick and broke the basement window to get inside. I saw a dead man lying on the floor in the basement. I figured that Toby had been there before me, and the old man surprised him, and they fought, and Toby killed him and fled when I knocked on the front door. Since the man was dead, I went ahead and robbed the place. Then I went out the back door and got in my car. I hit a neighbor's car but I kept going. I'm guilty of burglary and hit-and-run. But I swear to you, I didn't kill him."

Hammond threw her arms up in disbelief. "Your story is just so farfetched, Kermit. You're a guy who has spent virtually his entire adult life in prison, so you have no credibility."

"Well, I'm telling you the truth, and sometimes truth is stranger than fiction."

"Isn't it strange that we have all this evidence against you and no indication — not even microscopically — that anyone else broke into the house?"

"Maybe you people didn't do a very good job of gathering evidence."

"Oh, we have plenty. And it all points to you."

Godby folded his arms and squinted at her. "The only proof you have shows I was in the house the day Dietz was shot. But you have nothing to prove I was the one who killed him. I'm telling you, someone else murdered him. Probably Toby Brown. That's all I've got to say about this. I want to talk to a lawyer now."

When she left the interrogation room, Hammond received an update from Winthrop. "I found no blood on Godby's clothes or boots," the technician said. "He probably got rid of the clothes he wore that day. His work boots match the same general characteristics as the impressions in the carpeting of the upstairs bedroom. And we found two tiny shards of glass in between the shoelaces. They're consistent with the kind of glass from the smashed basement window."

"That's all well and good for a burglary conviction," said Hammond. "What we need is the murder weapon."

"Sorry to tell you this, Paula, but the Luger you recovered had never been fired. The bullets that killed Dr. Dietz didn't come from any of those other guns, either."

"No doubt he got rid of the Luger. In order to nail down a murder conviction, we need proof that Dr. Dietz was alive at the time of the burglary."

As Godby was being led away from the interrogation room by the officers, Hammond stopped them because she noticed something odd. He had been sweating so much that he had taken off his long-sleeved shirt, exposing bite marks on his left forearm. Pointing to his arm, she asked him, "How did you get those?"

"I, uh, got bit by a dog yesterday."

Those marks look like they were made by human teeth, Hammond thought. She knew each person has a unique bite because of the wear, age, and size of one's teeth. She played a hunch. "Kermit, a doctor should look at your arm, because that's a nasty bite and it looks infected."

Hammond summoned Newberry and explained what she wanted him to do. Newberry then examined Godby's arm and told him, "I definitely need to treat these dog bites." Newberry knew those were human bite marks, but he pretended otherwise. He put an antibacterial ointment on the "dog bites," making a big deal over how dangerous the infection could get if left untreated. Before the ointment was administered, Newberry got Godby's permission to take photos of the wound "as a way to see if the treatment is working or not." That was a fib.

After obtaining Dr. Dietz's dental records, the forensic examiner analyzed the size, shape, and alignment of the victim's teeth. Then he put a photo of the bite mark up on a board and laid a transparent sheet over it with a picture of Dietz's teeth. They matched.

"Your hunch was right, Paula," said Newberry. "I've just confirmed those bites were definitely made by Dr. Dietz. He probably surprised Godby, they got into a struggle, and Dr. Dietz bit him real hard. That's when the gun went off. Whether it was by accident or on purpose, I can't tell."

"It doesn't matter," she said. "Now we have proof that Dr. Dietz was alive when Godby broke into the house. That should get us the conviction we need to put him away for life. Justice will be a winner, and Godby will be a three-time loser."

Despite the overwhelming evidence, Godby pled not guilty and went to court. In 2006, the jury convicted him of first-degree murder and first-degree burglary. He was given the mandatory sentence of life in prison without parole.

The Case of the Dead Man Walking

Private eye Alex Weaver strode into the gleaming skyscraper of the insurance company headquarters in New York City. He had been summoned by the head of the fraud division to look into another suspicious case.

Weaver, a soft-spoken middle-aged detective, wore his usual tweed sport coat, jeans, and hiking boots. Owner of a Connecticut detective agency, he often was hired to probe a case when the insurance company suspected a death had been faked in order to collect on a policy. Weaver, who spoke four languages fluently, specialized in investigating alleged deaths in foreign countries.

The two biggest cases he had cracked involved millions of

dollars. A California man who had bought life insurance valued at $3.15 million supposedly died from a fall while hiking in the mountains of Chile. But when Weaver questioned the man's close friend who was the beneficiary (the person named in the policy to receive the money), the detective caught the friend in a series of lies. Tracking the friend's phone records, Weaver discovered the "dead" person had been in touch with the friend days after the alleged death. Both men eventually confessed to the fraud. A year later, a Florida woman submitted a death certificate to an insurance company on a $5 million policy, claiming her brother had died in a car accident in Colombia. Weaver investigated and proved the death certificate was a forgery.

Now, in 1998, he was about to take on the most challenging case of his career.

"I need you in Reynosa, Mexico," said company vice president John Littleton as he tossed Weaver a file. "His name is Grant Harrison Kennedy."

"Nice patriotic name — three presidents."

"Seven months ago, Kennedy bought a term-life policy from us for four million dollars. Last week, his wife, Rhonda Jefferds, filed a claim, saying Kennedy had died in a car accident while vacationing in Mexico.

"According to Kennedy's wife, he and a friend, Tim Welk, drove from Connecticut to Reynosa. Welk left him there and went on to Monterrey, 125 miles away. Two days later, on July 11, Kennedy rented a 1997 Chevrolet Suburban with plans to meet Welk in Monterrey and go mountain biking with mutual friends. The following day, Mexican federal police found Kennedy's burned-up car in a ravine off the Monterrey-Reynosa Freeway.

"The driver was all but incinerated. Among the charred remains, police found four human teeth, some bones, a Medic-Alert necklace containing the word *penicillin* and the name *G. Kennedy*, and a black wristwatch inscribed *To Grant — Love Rhonda*. But Mexican police found no mountain bike and no signs of a collision. Nevertheless, the medical examiner down there officially declared Kennedy dead."

"This smells fishy," said Weaver.

Littleton nodded. "Find out the truth, Alex. I'm not signing off on a four-million-dollar payment to the wife of a dead man who isn't dead."

Back at his office, Weaver studied the file. The case set off several warning bells that this was a classic fraud attempt. The death occurred in another country shortly after the insurance application was accepted. Kennedy, a 33-year-old financial consultant, was in debt, and the amount of insurance he obtained seemed way more than what he needed. And, conveniently for a swindler, the body was burned so badly there were few remains. *I'm going to need assistance on this one*, Weaver thought. *And I know just the person who can help me.*

A few days later, he was flying down to Mexico with Dr. Bartrum Banks, a distinguished professor and forensic anthropologist (a scientist who studies bones to determine how a person died and who that person was). With only a fragment of a skeleton, Banks often was able to tell police an unidentified dead person's age, race, and gender, and how and when he or she died.

His laboratory contained coffins of human skeletons, each representing different kinds of death, from gunshots to falls to old age. For many law-enforcement officials, Dr. Banks's bone collection became the last best chance to help solve a murder mystery.

Weaver knew the secrets of Banks's success were the bizarre experiments the professor carried out at the Body Farm, a fenced-in, three-acre plot where from 20 to 40 human bodies were kept. These corpses — usually donated to science or unclaimed from the county morgue — were exposed to the elements to see what happened. Banks would place bodies under cars, out in the open, in a house, under leaves, and in a pond. By studying how they decomposed, he could assist police in determining the time and cause of death.

"There's an old saying that dead men tell no tales, but that's not really true," the professor once told Weaver. "Dead men do tell tales — if you're trained to understand them."

When Weaver and Dr. Banks arrived in Reynosa, they were met by Lieutenant Roberto Salas, who was in charge of the initial investigation. On the way to showing them the wreck, which had been towed to a police impound area, Salas took them to the scene of the accident in the desert about 50 miles away. Pointing to a 20-foot-deep ravine about 30 feet off the road, he said, "We found the car still smoldering. It was resting on the driver's side."

"Were there any witnesses?" asked the detective.

"*No, señor*. There isn't much traffic at that hour of the night. About three in the morning, a passing motorist saw a ball of fire in the ravine. He stopped, watched the fire, and called out in the dark to see if anyone had survived. He didn't hear anyone. Then he left and drove on before he could call the police about five in the morning. We went out to investigate."

Weaver walked up and down the highway, studying the pavement. "That's odd. There are no skid marks."

"We think he fell asleep at the wheel and ran into the ravine," said Salas. "We talked to the staff at the hotel where Kennedy was staying in Reynosa. They said he had a few beers and left the hotel about ten P.M."

"He must have been somewhere else afterward because the accident happened at three A.M. only fifty miles away — a distance that would have taken him only an hour to drive," said the detective.

"That makes sense," said Salas. "We think he got drowsy and lost control of his car. When it went into the ravine, it caught fire and he was burned up. There's no body — just a few bones and some teeth. We have them in a box."

Although the accident scene had been disturbed by the police and the tow-truck operators, the Suburban's tire tracks were still visible in the desert soil.

"So your official report says he fell asleep at the wheel," said Weaver.

Salas nodded. "Yes. As you can see there are no skid marks."

"But even if you nod off, once your car goes off the road, the jolt would wake you up, and you'd slam on your brakes," said the detective. "There's absolutely no evidence of that here in the sand.

"Something else bothers me," Weaver added. "Judging from the area around the ravine, it doesn't seem the car was going fast enough to burst into flames upon impact. If the car left the road at a high rate of speed, it would be airborne, and yet the tracks show the wheels stayed on the ground all the way down into the ravine."

Walking behind a rock, Weaver spotted a part of the right-front headlight. It was cracked but still relatively intact. Pulling out a small magnifying glass he always carried with him, he examined the broken headlight. "Lieutenant, are you sure the accident happened while it was still dark?"

"I'm certain of it. The call came in at around five in the morning. Why do you ask?"

Weaver pointed to the filament, a threadlike conductor found in lightbulbs. "If such a bulb breaks while the lights are turned on, glass beads would form on the filament. But as you can see, that didn't happen here. The lights were off when this car crashed."

"Maybe his car had an electrical problem that caused him to lose control," said Salas.

"Or maybe the car was deliberately pushed into the ravine."

"I think it's time for us to examine the car," said Dr. Banks.

Salas took them to where the wreck was stored. Weaver walked around the burned-up Suburban and said, "When I first

25

start an investigation, I look at a potential crime scene and ask myself, *What does this scene tell me?* What does it tell you, Bartrum?"

"This was not an accident, that's for sure," Dr. Banks declared.

"Was it murder?"

"I don't know, Alex. What I can say with certainty is someone deliberately set this vehicle on fire. Look carefully at the rear."

When Weaver studied the right-rear panel of the vehicle, he noticed it was caved in, and parts were melted and scorched in such a way that he knew a high-intensity fire had started in the rear. "The fire wasn't from the engine burning up or a rupture of the gas tank," the detective said.

"Exactly," the professor agreed. "This isn't your average car fire. A car that runs off the road into a ravine doesn't burn up like this."

Turning to the lieutenant, Weaver asked, "Did you find any pieces of the bike?"

"No, *señor*."

"If the car burst into flames on impact, the bike would have burned, too, but some parts of it would have been found."

They examined Kennedy's few possessions that had been recovered from the accident. Dr. Banks fingered the Medic-Alert necklace the victim always wore to warn emergency-room physicians he was allergic to penicillin. "Alex, notice anything strange about this necklace?"

"Besides the fact that it survived such an intense fire and just happened to have Kennedy's name on it? I see that it's unclasped and not broken."

"Exactly. It's highly unlikely the necklace would become unfastened on its own. Assume that he started the fire. He would have taken off the necklace . . ."

"Because he wanted to leave it in the car as proof he was the victim who had died," Weaver said, finishing Dr. Banks's sentence.

"Exactly. And, Alex, he would have waited until the fire had died down enough so it wouldn't burn up the necklace."

"What a coincidence the only other possession that survived the fire was his engraved watch. In a fire this hot, part of the watch should have melted, but it didn't. He probably tossed it into the fire the same time he did his necklace."

Like archaeologists excavating an ancient site, the investigators carefully sifted through the wreckage looking for clues. Within a few minutes, Weaver held up a part of a burned shoe. On the bottom of the sole were some impressed letters, most of which were illegible. "I can barely make it out," he said. "It looks like OCKP. What do you suppose that means?"

Dr. Banks smiled and lifted his left leg so Weaver could see the name on the bottom of the professor's shoe.

"Rockport," Weaver read. "Kennedy must have been wearing Rockport shoes. Hard to believe the shoes wouldn't have been incinerated."

"They're good shoes, Alex, and that's the reason I wear them. The shoe survived because it was tossed into the fire as an afterthought."

"The evidence is saying Kennedy faked his own death."

Dr. Banks held up his hand and said, "Before we jump to what appears to be an obvious conclusion, we must determine if the bones in the car are his or not." After gently picking up pieces inside the wreckage for several minutes, Dr. Banks shouted, "Aha! Look what I've found." With his tweezers, he held up a scorched round bone about the size of the cap of a peanut-butter jar.

"What is it, Bartrum?" asked Weaver.

"A piece of the top of a skull. Clearly the skull had broken apart in the fire, but why would I have found it so far over on the passenger side under the glove compartment?"

"Maybe he wasn't wearing a seat belt and fell toward the passenger side on impact?"

"The car has air bags," said Dr. Banks. "It would have held him in place. Another fact is that when the car hit the ditch, it ended up leaning on the driver's side, yet this bone was on the passenger side. This indicates to me the body was placed there after the crash and before the fire was set."

They continued to examine the car until they had collected several more bone fragments and teeth. They returned to the police station and spread out all the human remains for a closer look.

Dr. Banks held up several vertebrae — some of the 33 bony segments that make up the spinal column. "Alex, what happens to your bones the older you get?"

"They wear out."

"Exactly. I can tell in a general sense the age of a skeleton by examining its bones. Look at these vertebrae here. See how worn they are? These are the bones of someone in his sixties or seventies who suffered from arthritis. These are not the bones of a man in his thirties who likes mountain biking."

"If they're not Grant Kennedy's, then whose are they?"

Dr. Banks examined the teeth and a partial jawbone. "I don't know, but I can tell you this much. This victim isn't white."

"How do you know that?"

The professor pointed to his own teeth. "When you and I bite down, we have an overbite with the upper teeth in front of the lower ones. Native Americans have an edge-to-edge bite in the incisor region [any of the four front teeth in the upper or lower jaw]. As a result, they get a lot of wear on the biting surface of the back teeth. The remains are from a Native American, definitely a male and probably about five and a half feet tall."

"Did Kennedy find an old skeleton and throw it in the car?" Weaver asked.

"No. I can tell from the fractures of the bones they belonged to someone who died recently — either the night of the accident or shortly before. We might not know who he is, Alex, but at least we can prove he's not Grant Kennedy."

"So Kennedy killed him and placed him here before setting the car on fire . . ."

"Or he robbed a fresh grave."

At Weaver's request, Lieutenant Salas asked law-enforcement officials throughout the area for any reports of a disturbed grave or a missing older man around the time of the accident. The next day, Salas told the two investigators, "The only missing persons we know about are two teenage girls and a man in his twenties. No one has heard of any robberies of graves, either. The only report that comes close is from the caretaker of the local mausoleum [a structure that houses burial vaults in its walls]. He chased off an SUV the same night as the accident."

Dr. Banks and Weaver looked at each other and nodded. "Let's talk to the caretaker," said the detective.

At the mausoleum, the investigators questioned Emilio Hurtado. He told them, "This place is locked up at night. I sleep in the little house at the far end of the grounds. About midnight, I heard a loud noise by the back gate. When I got there, a large white car was speeding away."

"Was it a Chevrolet Suburban?"

"Sí, señor."

"Then what happened?" the detective asked.

"When I reached the gate, it was unlocked — and I know I locked it before going to bed. I looked around and saw a statue had been knocked over and smashed, so I called the police. I checked everything the next morning. Nothing was stolen."

"Were any burial vaults disturbed?" asked Dr. Banks.

"No, señor."

"Was anyone interred [laid to rest] earlier that day?"

"Yes, I believe so." Hurtado checked his ledger. "Ah, yes. Manuel Ortiz. Nice man. A bricklayer."

"Describe him for me, please," said the professor.

"Short. Stocky. In his sixties. Half Mexican, half Cherokee."

"After Ortiz's coffin was put in the vault in the wall, did you seal it up that day?" Weaver asked.

"Of course, *señor.*"

"Can we see his vault?"

Moments later, the investigators were examining the outside of the vault. "How do you seal the vault?" asked Weaver.

"With concrete, of course," the caretaker replied.

The detective took out the Swiss Army knife he always carried and chipped away at the seal. "This isn't grout or concrete around the edges. It's caulking — like the kind that goes around windows."

"Impossible," Hurtado declared. "We sealed it with concrete."

"See for yourself. The whole vault is sealed with window caulking the same color as the concrete." He pulled out the caulking. "The burial vault was sealed with concrete, but someone chiseled it out before it became too hard." Turning to the professor, he said, "Bartrum, I don't think anyone is in the coffin."

After convincing the authorities, the investigators watched as the police pulled out the coffin of Manuel Ortiz and opened it up. As the detective suspected, it was empty.

"Now we know who was burned up in Kennedy's car," said Weaver. "Kennedy needed a fresh body, so he waited until someone died. When Ortiz was interred here, Kennedy sneaked in, broke the concrete seal before it set, pulled out the coffin, and stole the body, no doubt with the help of an accomplice. They probably knocked over the statue when they were carrying the body out. And they drove off just as the caretaker arrived."

"Well, at least part of your mystery is solved," said Dr. Banks.

"Yeah. Now the big question is: Where is Kennedy?"

Back in the United States, Dr. Banks returned to his laboratory. Weaver presented the insurance company with proof that Kennedy hadn't died in the crash in Mexico. The insurance claim filed by Kennedy's wife was rejected. The detective, with Dr. Banks's help, had just saved the company $4 million.

Weaver turned his information over to police because this was now a criminal matter. But for the next two years, the authorities were unable to locate Kennedy or his friend.

The detective focused on other cases. Then one day, Dirk Emerson, one of the investigators at the agency, knocked on Weaver's office door and said, "Remember the fake death case with the guy whose name was made up of presidents?"

"Of course — Grant Harrison Kennedy. What about him?"

"Well, I'm doing a background check on a guy being considered for the post of chief financial officer for a company, and his name is also three presidents — Carter Truman Wilson. It's not often you run across someone with three presidential names."

"Let me look at your file." Weaver compared the background information he had on Kennedy with the one Emerson had compiled on Wilson. Certain past addresses were identical.

And so were the names of people listed as references. Weaver looked at the photos in each file. Wilson had a different hairstyle and was somewhat heavier than Kennedy, but there was no doubt in Weaver's mind Wilson and Kennedy were one and the same.

"Dirk, you might be in for a Christmas bonus this year!"

Early the next morning, Weaver drove to the Boston address Wilson had put on his résumé, and he ran a license-plate check on the car parked in the driveway. It was owned by Rhonda Jefferds, Kennedy's wife.

Then a warm, satisfying feeling welled up in the detective's gut. From across the street, he saw the faker in the flesh, a con artist who had been sought after by police — a very much alive Grant Harrison Kennedy.

After watching Kennedy walk out of the house and get into the car, Weaver followed him to an office parking lot and called the police. Before giving them the information they needed to make an arrest, he told them with great pleasure, "I'm tailing a dead man walking."

Grant Harrison Kennedy was arrested in 2000. He pled guilty to insurance fraud and was sentenced to five years in federal prison. He confessed that he and his friend Tim Welk stole the body of Manuel Ortiz and put it in the Suburban. Welk, driving his own car, followed Kennedy in the Suburban to a secluded spot on the highway. After Kennedy took out his mountain bike, they pushed the Suburban into a ravine, splashed the vehicle with gasoline, and set it on fire. Welk drove off and waited for him about a mile down the road while Kennedy remained behind to make sure the car and body had burned up. After the fire began to weaken, he tossed in his watch, necklace, and shoes so they would be discovered. Then he rode off on his bike and met up with Welk, who sneaked him back into the United States where he began his new life as Carter Truman Wilson.

Only Kennedy's friend and wife knew of the scheme. Welk was never found. But Rhonda Jefferds was arrested for her part in the plot. However, she received a suspended sentence in exchange for her testimony.

The
Case of the
Floating
Corpse

It's the most horrifying thing I've ever seen in my life," shuddered retired judge Jack Longwood, visibly upset at the ghastly sight.

Brevard (Florida) County sheriff's detective Peter Gamble nodded. "Yeah, I know what you mean. I've been in law enforcement for more than thirty years, and I still don't get used to it."

They were standing at the edge of the Indian River in the backyard of the judge's waterfront home on Merritt Island on a steamy July morning in 2000. Already sweating through his white Mexican shirt that draped over his ample belly, the portly detective took off his straw hat and waved it in front of him to cool off. He and the judge stared at the decomposing corpse of a young woman as it was being retrieved from the shallow water by a recovery team.

"I was working in my yard when I saw something floating in the water," said Longwood. "I couldn't believe it was a body. It's pretty obvious she was murdered."

White duct tape was wrapped around her head, covering her eyes, nose, and mouth. Her hands and feet were bound by marine rope. Plastic grocery bags were attached to her feet and fastened with a rubbery cord.

"Why would there be supermarket bags on her feet?" the judge asked.

"My guess is they were filled with ballast, something heavy to weigh down the body," Gamble replied. "The bags are split open, which indicates the ballast was so heavy it broke them, causing the body to float to the surface."

"I hope you catch whoever did this, Detective," said Longwood.

"Judge, I always get my man. Always."

The veteran cop, who preferred to work alone, had a flawless record of nabbing killers. He had solved every homicide case in which he was the lead investigator. A savvy detective who had no home life — he had been divorced for years — Gamble practically lived at the sheriff's office, willing to put in long days to crack a case.

Hours after discovery of the floating corpse, Gamble visited Dr. Howard Engel, the medical examiner who had conducted a preliminary inspection of the body. The victim was a woman in her twenties with long brown hair and blue eyes, five feet six inches tall and weighing 130 pounds. She had been dead for between 48 and 72 hours.

"In my opinion, the victim died from asphyxia [a condition caused by lack of oxygen] either by suffocation from the tape over her nose and mouth or by drowning," Dr. Engel said. "I found no fractures, entrance or exit wounds [from a bullet], or injuries from a sharp object. There is a dent in her skull that could have been caused by being struck by a blunt object, but not hard enough to kill her."

"Someone probably knocked her out and taped up her nose and mouth so she couldn't breathe," said Gamble. "Then she was tossed in the water."

Back at the sheriff's office, the detective sifted through recent missing persons reports. One that had been filed the day before seemed a likely match — 22-year-old Meadow Morgan of nearby Satellite Beach who had been reported missing by her mother, Lynn Morgan. A deputy brought Mrs. Morgan to the morgue where she nearly collapsed from anguish after positively identifying the body as her daughter. Dental records later confirmed it was the young woman.

Shortly after Mrs. Morgan recovered from her shock, Gamble questioned her. "When did you last see Meadow?" he asked.

"About two-thirty A.M. three days ago, Thursday. She had been living with me ever since my divorce last year. I own a two-bedroom townhouse off Atlantic Boulevard. Around two in the morning, her cell phone rang and woke me up. I dozed off for a moment, and then I heard Meadow showering and drying her hair. Her phone rang again and she talked for a short bit. I'm a nurse on the early-morning shift, so I had to get up anyway. It was close to three A.M. We passed each other in the hallway, and she had on her makeup and was in a sundress. I asked her where she was going, and she said she was meeting up with some friends. . . ."

"At three in the morning?"

"Well, truth be told, Detective, Meadow loved to party. She worked the four-to-midnight shift at the Sage and Sand Restaurant as a hostess. So it wasn't that unusual for her to be out all night. She kissed me good-bye and said she'd see me later that day." Mrs. Morgan let out a sorrowful moan. "I never saw her again." After composing herself, she said, "When I left for work, her car was still there. I assumed a friend had picked her up."

"Did she have a boyfriend or ex-boyfriend?"

"She was seeing someone — Scott Miles. He manages a tire store in Melbourne. I've never met him, but she said he was nice. They had been dating about a month."

"And before him?"

"Oh, my. There were several. She had an active social life. She had been going with Ben Helton for more than a year, but they broke up about six months ago. He's a charter-boat captain. They still see each other from time to time, but she said it's strictly a friendship thing now."

"Did she ever fear for her life or say if one of her boyfriends was ever violent?"

"No. She told me some of her dates turned out to be jerks, but that's all."

"I'll need a list of all her friends and boyfriends."

"Do you think one of them killed her?"

"Mrs. Morgan, in the vast majority of cases, the victim knew the killer."

Gamble went to the tire store to interview Miles, but a worker there said Miles was so grief-stricken over Meadow's death that he took the day off. The detective drove to Miles's apartment and found him in a T-shirt and shorts, unshaven, hair uncombed, sitting in a chair, staring with bloodshot eyes at nothing. He was mindlessly turning over a driver's license in his hands.

"We were having such a good time together," Miles whimpered. "I can't believe she's gone."

"Where were you between midnight and noon on Thursday?"

"I was asleep here until about six, and then I went to work."

"When did you last see Meadow?"

"Tuesday night. That's her night off. We went to the Blue Parrot until about eleven and then we came back to my place. Later I drove her home."

"What do you have in your hands?"

Without looking up, Miles held up the driver's license. Gamble plucked it from his fingers and read the name. "Scott, what are you doing with Meadow's driver's license?"

Miles rubbed his eyes and replied, "She asked me to hold it for her because she didn't have pockets on her dress, and she wasn't carrying a purse. I forgot to give it back. I found it in my pants the next morning, and I called her about it. She told me to hold on to it because we were planning on seeing each other Thursday."

"When did you last speak to her?"

"I talked to her Wednesday before she went to work. We were supposed to meet for lunch at the Bahama Hut on Thursday, but she didn't show. I kept trying to reach her that afternoon, but she never answered her cell phone."

"Do you know why anyone would want to kill her?"

He shook his head. "Everyone liked Meadow."

"Was she dating other men while she was going out with you?"

"Probably. Like I said, everyone liked her."

"Did she ever tell you of being harmed or that she felt threatened?"

"No, although she mentioned to me and others that her old boyfriend Ben Helton got drunk one night and hit her. But that supposedly happened six months ago."

"Scott, look at me. I need a straight answer from you. Did you kill Meadow?"

"No, of course not," Miles replied firmly while locking eyes with the detective. "I really liked her. A lot. I would never harm her."

Gamble wasn't so sure. He didn't trust anyone, especially victims' boyfriends. He found it strange that Miles would have Meadow's driver's license. "Mind if I take a look around your apartment?"

Miles waved his hand in consent.

"While I'm looking around, write down the names of all her friends." The detective spent a half hour rummaging through the apartment but didn't find anything suspicious.

Gamble checked the phone records of outgoing and incoming calls on Meadow's cell phone. Miles had called at the times he had stated. The records showed the last two calls Meadow received the night she disappeared came from Ben Helton. He called her at 1:58 A.M. for two minutes and then again at 2:23 A.M. for one minute. No other calls were made or answered on her phone after that call.

Gamble now focused his investigation on Helton, who reluctantly agreed to talk to the detective at the sheriff's office.

"I met Meadow about a year and a half ago," Helton said. "We dated for nearly a year, but broke up because she cheated on me. I was pretty angry with her, but I got over it. We kept hanging out at the same places, so we remained friends. She was dating other guys, and I had a new girlfriend."

"When did you last see Meadow?"

"A week ago. I stopped in at the Sage and Sand for a late-night bite to eat."

"When did you last talk to her?"

"I called her early Thursday morning, around two A.M. I was out with friends, and they told me she was telling people I had abused her during our relationship. I was furious. So I called her and said, 'What's going on? Why are you lying about me? If my girlfriend hears this, it could ruin things for me.' Meadow denied saying bad things about me and promised to tell people I never harmed her. I went home about two-thirty and called Meadow again just to thank her. That's the last time I spoke to her."

"Can you think of any reason why someone would kill her?"

Helton hesitated and said, "You can't explain why someone would tie up a woman and throw her in the river."

Well, well, well. I definitely have a strong suspect, thought Gamble. *He either killed her or knows who did.* No one in the sheriff's office had publicly revealed that the victim had been tied up. *What I need is strong forensic evidence to prove he's the killer. Either that or a confession.*

"Ben, were you involved in any way in Meadow Morgan's murder?"

Helton huffed, "My position is I didn't do anything."

"Okay, then you should be willing to sign a consent form authorizing a search of your house."

Helton reluctantly signed the form.

Later that day, Gamble and crime-scene technician Carly Holtzman searched Helton's home. While looking in the garage, the detective found a black rubbery cord hanging from a shelf as if it had recently been cut. The cord, designed to attach screen fabric to door or window frames, was the same kind that had been wrapped around the plastic bags on the feet of the corpse.

Inside the house, Gamble examined Helton's bedroom. In a dresser, he recovered a partially used roll of white duct tape. When he walked into the kitchen with the tape, he showed it to Helton and asked, "Do you always keep duct tape in your dresser?"

Helton's mouth dropped open. He stammered and said, "I, uh, had it in my pocket and forgot to leave it on my boat, so I tossed it in the drawer."

While searching the kitchen, Gamble found several tan plastic bags from Publix, a popular grocery chain in Florida. The bags, which had BABY CLUB printed on them, were identical to those on the victim's feet.

During an examination of Helton's car, Holtzman recovered several long brown hairs on the passenger seat and floor. She also seized some hairs for comparison purposes from Helton's dog, Chewbacca, a Rottweiler–German shepherd mix. The pet had been a gift from Meadow to Helton when they were dating.

Next, investigators examined Helton's boat, which was docked in a canal behind his house. Holtzman picked up two long brown hairs from the deck and a small portion of matted brown hair from a fishing-rod holder.

Gamble noticed that a retractable boat light on a pole above the captain's chair had been sheared off. "How did that happen?" he asked Helton.

"It's kind of embarrassing," Helton admitted. "A couple of weeks ago, I was returning home from the Blue Parrot late at night and I wasn't paying attention to the tides. It was high tide when I went under the Mathers Bridge, and I forgot to lower the light and it broke off."

Gamble measured the distance from the waterline to the spot where the pole was snapped off. It was seven and a half feet.

Moments after the detective left the boat, he spotted Terry Ripulski, Helton's deckhand, who had been questioned the day before. "Tell me something, Terry," said the detective. "What is the shortest water route to Merritt Island from here?"

"Well, you'd travel north on the canal from here and into the Indian River."

"Would you go under any really low bridges?"

"The only low one is the swing bridge — Mathers Bridge."

"What is the clearance under it?"

"It ranges from about six feet at high tide to seven and a half feet at low tide."

"So you have to lower the light on Helton's boat before going under the bridge, right?"

"Of course, Detective, or else you'll snap it off."

"When did the light break on Helton's boat?"

"Huh? It's not broken, and I would know because it's my job to lower it."

"When was the last time you were onboard?"

"Over the weekend."

Gamble drove to Mathers Bridge and inspected its south side. A two-inch section had clearly been chipped as if by some impact, such as a tall light from a boat.

Scanning a tide chart, Gamble learned the tide was at its lowest around 4 A.M. on the morning Meadow disappeared. *If Helton was using the boat at that time to get out into the Indian River and he forgot to lower the light, it would have broken off at Mathers Bridge at seven and a half feet from the waterline — exactly the height that I found it snapped off.*

Meanwhile, a diver from the sheriff's office, who had been dispatched by Gamble, recovered a small piece of plastic marine rope 10 feet under the canal near the seawall behind Helton's house. The rope had a unique red-and-white diamond pattern — the exact same color and design as the rope used to tie up Meadow's body. The diver also looked for pieces of the broken light under Mathers Bridge but didn't find any.

Within days, Gamble heard back from forensic experts who had examined the recovered evidence. Holtzman gave him the facts about the grocery bags.

"There were three million plastic Publix bags with BABY CLUB printed on them," she reported. "Publix started using them last month."

"Three million?" moaned Gamble. "That doesn't help my case any."

"Don't rush to judgment, Detective. The bags bore quality-control numbers that showed when and where they were manufactured, and even the specific operator who made them. The bags you took from Helton's kitchen and the bags recovered from the victim's feet were produced by the same employee on the same machine at the bag-making plant in June. Bags with different dates produced by different operators are randomly scattered throughout the Publix distribution system — yet you found bags in Helton's kitchen that had identical markings with those found on the victim."

"Well, I guess that *does* help my case," Gamble said.

"Now let's talk about the rope used on the victim and what the diver found. Both ropes have the same unusual double-diamond pattern and are consistent in every manner. I tried to locate similar rope in the area, but I was unsuccessful. An assistant manager of Dean's Marine Supply told me in his ten years in the business he had never before seen rope with that specific pattern. He tried to locate the pattern through most of the U.S. manufacturers, but was unsuccessful."

"Were you able to match up the cut ends of the rope found under Helton's dock and the rope used on Meadow's body?"

"Pretty close, but not with the certainty you would need in court."

Gamble then heard from Janet Solomon, a microanalyst (a person who conducts microscopic testing of objects) with the Florida Department of Law Enforcement. She compared the white duct tape found on the victim with the duct tape recovered from Helton's bedroom. "The two pieces of tape were of the same type and same grade, and were most probably made by the same manufacturer," she explained. "Only four to six per cent of the duct tape manufactured in the United States is white, but I've been unable to pinpoint the tape's specific manufacturer."

"Can you prove the tape on the body came from the roll I found in Helton's home?"

"I couldn't conclusively match the ends of the tape with the tape on the roll. Nor could I get any fingerprints or DNA off the tape wrapped over the victim's head."

"What can you tell me about the rubbery cord I found in the Heltons' garage?" asked Gamble.

"My analysis shows the cord in the garage and the cord on the victim's body were produced by the same manufacturer, in the same plant, and on the same machine."

Next, Gamble talked with Mark Waverly, a trace-evidence examiner with the FBI. He compared samples of Meadow's hair with hair recovered from Helton's boat and car. "The samples showed the same microscopic characteristics as those from the victim," Waverly said. "Not only are they the exact same color, but I've concluded that less than two percent of the U.S. population could be the source of the hair.

"I also found artificial-color treatment on the hair, which is noteworthy because, according to her mother, Meadow had colored her hair the day before she disappeared."

"My case is getting stronger and stronger," said the detective.

"There's more," Waverly said. "Dog hairs were found on the rope and tape used to bind the victim's body. I compared them to samples of hair taken from Helton's dog. The hair on the tape and rope bore the same characteristics as the dog's."

Based on the evidence and interviews with Meadow's friends, Gamble created a theory of what happened in the early morning hours of July 20, 2000: After an evening of drinking with friends, Helton fumed over learning that Meadow was telling others he had abused her when they were dating. Because he was involved with a new girlfriend, Helton feared Meadow's statements would ruin his new relationship. He was determined to keep Meadow quiet at any cost. So Helton called Meadow on her cell phone and sweet-talked her into letting him pick her up for a face-to-face chat over drinks. Sometime during the next few hours, Helton argued with Meadow and knocked her out. He covered her mouth and nose with duct tape and she suffocated. He bound her body with rope and tied grocery bags filled with rocks to her feet. He took the corpse out in his boat — shearing off his boat light on Mathers Bridge in his haste — and dumped the body into the Indian River near Merritt Island.

Flanked by two sheriff's deputies, Gamble arrested Helton. Defiant, the suspect sneered, "You don't have enough evidence to convict me."

"Oh, you're so wrong," countered the detective. "You see, Ben, when it comes to murder, I always get my man."

Ben Helton pled not guilty and went to trial in 2003. The jury took less than four hours to reach a verdict — guilty of kidnapping and first-degree felony murder. Helton was sentenced to life in prison without the possibility of parole.

— The —
Case of the
Telltale
Ring

Nebraska State Patrol investigator Richard Havel sensed the uneasiness and fear brewing in the small farming community. There hadn't been a murder in the county in at least 10 years. Now here he was about to probe a double homicide at a quaint and neat farmhouse two miles from town.

Havel walked past dozens of stunned folks who had gathered to grieve in front of the freshly painted white house. They spoke in hushed but nervous voices, some clutching hankies to wipe their tears. He felt bad that the peace and security these decent people had enjoyed their whole lives had been shattered, maybe forever.

As he stepped into the home the day after Easter 2006, all Havel knew was that 58-year-old Warren Strickland and his

55-year-old wife Sharon — well-respected, lifelong residents — had been mercilessly slain in their bedroom during the night. Their bodies had been discovered in the afternoon by their son, David. When Sheriff Bob Bailey examined the crime scene, he immediately had asked for Havel's assistance.

"We have a heartbreaking mess here," Bailey told the veteran detective. "The medical examiner thinks they were killed sometime after ten last night."

"How did the killer get inside?"

"You mean killers. Someone took the screen off a kitchen window, lifted the window, and slipped inside. We were able to get a good palm print off the glass. We think the perp unlocked the back door and let one or more people inside."

"What makes you say that?"

"Follow me." The sheriff led Havel to the top of the stairs where Warren Strickland had been killed. "Someone with a shotgun went up here with an accomplice. Warren must have heard them, got out of bed, surprised them, and was shot. Look at the pattern of the blood on the wall."

Havel noticed most of the wall was splattered with blood except for a clean area that formed the shape of a person.

"One of the perps was standing off to the side of the shooter when Warren was shot," Bailey said. "The perp got sprayed with Warren's blood and blocked part of the wall from getting splattered.

"We think the second perp was a shooter, too. We found three spent shells from a twelve-gauge shotgun on the stairway and a live shell from a .410 shotgun at the top of the stairs. I doubt if one person was carrying two shotguns."

The sheriff motioned for Havel to step into the bedroom. "When Warren was killed, the blast woke up Sharon. The shooters went into the bedroom and shot her right after she picked up the phone by her bed."

"Was anything taken?" Havel asked.

"Nothing that we can tell. The house wasn't ransacked and drawers weren't opened. Their son, David, has gone through the rooms and didn't see anything missing. It's such a needless killing. The victims were good people, church people."

"Any family problems?"

"They're a tight-knit family that always has Sunday dinner together."

"What other evidence have you found, Sheriff?"

"We discovered a strange silver-and-red pipe in the driveway. The Stricklands didn't smoke, and none of the family members do, either. There were fourteen people at the house for Easter yesterday. Surely someone would have seen the pipe if it had been there before the murders. We think it belongs to the perps. We're having it checked for fingerprints and DNA."

Havel walked through the house looking for clues. Even though it was daylight, he shined a flashlight along the floors — a technique he often used because the beam sometimes helped him spot a clue. Today was one of those days. Slowly moving his flashlight on the kitchen floor, a glint caught his eye. He got down on his hands and knees and, to his surprise, found a shiny gold ring under the table. It had gone unnoticed by the deputies during their initial search.

Wearing rubber gloves, the investigator picked up the ring and studied it. Having no nicks or scratches, it looked new and was engraved with the words *Love always. Cori and Ryan.*

"You know the Strickland family pretty well, right?" Havel asked Bailey.

"I know all of them, sure."

"Who are Cori and Ryan?"

Bailey thought a moment and replied, "Never heard of them."

"Mrs. Strickland kept an extremely clean house," Havel said. "Everything here is spotless, even after just hosting a big Easter dinner. Yet, I find a gold ring under the table with engraved names that don't match anyone in the family. I wonder if it was worn by one of the killers."

"We'll ask the family if those names ring a bell. We'll also run a name check of anyone named Cori or Ryan in the area."

After searching every room, Havel walked outside and examined the well-manicured yard. A hedge of evergreen shrubs bordered the home. Havel peered behind the hedge at the rich soil that separated the grass from the foundation. To the right of the back doorstep, he noticed two fresh footprints from a pair of sneakers.

"The footprints might be from one of the killers," Havel told Bailey. "He or she was probably hiding by the back door, waiting for the accomplice to break into the house through the kitchen window. Have one of your people take a picture of the footprints and also get a plaster cast of them."

Havel then interviewed farmers who lived from a quarter-mile to a half-mile apart along the gravel country road. No one saw or heard anything unusual the previous night.

"I'm devastated," said neighbor Donald van de Kamp. "It's kind of bone-chilling. I can't believe it. Warren was always so generous, and Sharon was, too. She made lots of cakes for people for the big events in their lives, like birthdays and weddings and baptisms. I can't imagine why anybody would want to hurt the Stricklands."

Three days later, Havel and Bailey attended the funeral service of the slain couple, which drew more than 3,000 people to the local high-school gym — the only place big enough to hold everyone. Sheriff's deputies took video of the service, believing that the unknown murderers might be in the crowd.

The crime lab obtained DNA off the ring and the pipe so the samples could be compared with the DNA of any possible suspects. Meanwhile, Bailey and the deputies continued to question friends and relatives of the victims, following up on several leads.

Havel, however, focused his attention on the gold ring. The investigator took it to jewelers in the area, hoping someone might recognize it. He learned the type of ring was a fairly common one sold by a chain of jewelry stores in the Midwest. At Havel's urging, the chain sent out a request to all its stores in a 12-state area to examine their records over the past year to see if anyone sold a ring with that specific inscription.

Eight days after the murder, Havel received startling news in a phone call from Bailey. "We've got two suspects in custody in the Strickland murders," the sheriff announced. "One of them is their nephew, Luke Mathews, and the other is his cousin, Sam Nichols, the son of a friend of the family. They both were at the funeral. I'm pretty confident they did it."

Havel arrived at the sheriff's office and watched from a two-way mirror as Bailey relentlessly grilled each suspect separately.

"We have eyewitnesses who heard you talking about getting even with Warren Strickland because he had fired you a few weeks ago," Bailey said to Mathews, a 28-year-old handyman with a low IQ.

"He was sore at me because I backed his truck into a post," Mathews explained. "It was the second time it happened. He said maybe I'd be better off working elsewhere, and I said okay. I was angry with him, but I wouldn't kill Uncle Warren."

Shoving his face within an inch of his nose, Bailey mocked him. "So these people who heard you at the Husker's Bar and Grill just made stuff up about you bad-mouthing Warren?"

"All I said was I deserved another chance, and I was upset that Uncle Warren wouldn't give it to me."

"Luke, people saw you and Sam leave together the night of the murder."

"Sam drove me home. That's all."

"Where were you on Easter night from ten P.M. to six in the morning?"

"Asleep at home. My parents can tell you that."

"Did you murder your aunt and uncle? Did Sam murder them?"

"No, I didn't. And no, Sam didn't. We didn't kill anyone."

Bailey's questioning of Nichols, a 22-year-old mechanic, also didn't get any satisfying answers. And neither suspect claimed to know who Cori and Ryan were.

After the interrogation, Bailey told Havel, "I'm close to breaking Luke and getting him to confess. We've recovered twelve-gauge shotguns from both their homes and we're having them tested. We're also comparing their DNA to the DNA on the ring and the pipe. We're not sure why the palm print on the kitchen window doesn't match with either suspect. Maybe there's a third person."

"What about the footprints?"

"It's the same size shoe Nichols wears, but we haven't found a shoe of his that fits the tread in the footprints."

The following day, after hours of relentless questioning and dozens of denials, Mathews finally confessed that he and Nichols had killed the Stricklands, just as Bailey suspected. But Mathews was too distraught and worn out to give precise details of how or why they murdered the couple. However, two days after the sheriff publicly announced the case was solved, Mathews withdrew his confession.

"Do you really think Mathews and Nichols did it?" Havel asked Bailey.

Annoyed by the question, the sheriff snapped, "Of course, I do. They have weak alibis, they were heard making insulting remarks about Warren Strickland, and Nichols's shoes are the same size as the footprints. They both attended the Stricklands' funeral, and after I watched the video of the service, those two didn't seem all that broken up over the deaths. And, don't forget, we found shotguns — the possible murder weapons — in their homes. Our tests showed the guns had been fired recently."

When Havel was leaving the sheriff's office, he bumped into Mathews's attorney, Emily Bean. "I know you hear this all the time, Detective, but my client is innocent," she asserted.

"He confessed to the murders," said Havel.

"That confession was made after hours of mental strain," Bean contended. "Luke has been learning-disabled his whole life, and his intellectual abilities are well below ninety-five percent of the adult population. Luke has never been in trouble with the law before and has always been respectful and trusting of the police. He volunteered to meet with them to help in any way he could with the investigation. But Bailey and his men were convinced he did it, and kept pressuring him until he was psychologically worn out and willing to say anything to stop the interrogation."

Bean clutched his arm and said, "Detective, I've heard you are a decent man. Don't quit on this case because you think you've caught the murderers. The wrong men are in jail, and the real killers are still loose out there."

"Miss Bean, I assure you I haven't stopped working on this case. I'll go wherever the evidence leads me. If it points to your client, then too bad for him. If it points elsewhere, then I'll do my level best to catch the perpetrators."

"That's all I ask, Detective."

Havel began having real doubts that Mathews and Nichols committed murder after tests showed their DNA didn't match the DNA from the ring and the pipe. Microscopic analysis of the barrels of their shotguns proved the weapons were not used in the murders. In fact, there was no hard evidence linking either man to the crime.

Two weeks after the arrests, Havel received a phone call from a jeweler in Madison, Wisconsin. She told him she had sold the gold ring to Cori Willet of Beaver Dam, Wisconsin, the previous November.

Thinking Willet might be involved in or have knowledge of the murders, Havel called her, pretending to be a jeweler. "I was given the ring by a Good Samaritan who found it in the road," he lied. "Did you lose such a ring?"

"Oh, it's sweet someone would go through all that trouble to find its owner," Willet replied. "But, no, I didn't lose the ring. You should check with Ryan Kegle."

"Who's he?"

"My ex-boyfriend. When we were going together, I gave him the ring for Christmas, but then we broke up two months ago. I don't know if he gave it away or threw it away or lost it."

Now suspecting that Kegle, who also lived in Beaver Dam, was connected to the murders, Havel phoned Sheriff Norman Cedarquist of Dodge County, Wisconsin. Havel told Cedarquist about the Nebraska murders and the ring's possible link to them. "So, Sheriff, do you know anything about Ryan Kegle?"

"He's not the killer you're looking for," Cedarquist declared. "Hold on, while I get the report." A minute later, the sheriff returned to the phone and said, "On April 15, Kegle reported his 2002 red Dodge pickup was stolen. Among the items he listed as in the truck were a toolbox, fishing gear, and the ring you described, which he kept in the glove compartment. Also taken from his home were a twelve-gauge pump-action shotgun and a box of shells and some money.

"The truck was found abandoned April 19 in Louisiana. A teenage couple — Julia Rudner and Gage Foster — were arrested a week later on auto-theft charges. They live in the county. Rudner is only seventeen and doesn't have a criminal record, so she's free on bond. Foster is nineteen, and he's had several run-ins with the law — petty theft and assault — so he remains in our jail.

"You definitely want to question them about the double homicide. They haven't said much to us, but they did admit stealing the truck and going on a road trip. They said they robbed a farmhouse in Iowa and another one in Nebraska, looking for money to pay for food, gas, and motel rooms. They never said anything about murder."

The next day, after a tiring 500-mile drive to Wisconsin, Havel went straight to the Dodge County jail to interview Foster. "I've already admitted to theft and burglary," the suspect told him. "But as for murder, I don't know what you're talking about."

Rudner, who had been living on her own for a year, also denied any involvement in the Strickland murders when Havel questioned her.

Asked about the ring, she said, "I opened the glove compartment of the pickup we stole and found the ring. It was pretty and I put it on. It was too big for my fingers, so I wore it on my thumb. At some point in all the excitement during the robberies, I lost the ring."

"Did you or Gage ever use a silver-and-red pipe?"

"Yeah. We took turns smoking it throughout our trip, but we lost it somewhere."

She submitted to a palm print, which turned out to be identical to the one on the Stricklands' kitchen window.

Sheriff Cedarquist received a faxed report from the sheriff of Guthrie County, Iowa, of a break-in at a farm in the early morning hours of Easter Sunday. Taken in the burglary were a .410 single-shot shotgun, ammunition, cash, and a U.S. Navy belt buckle.

Under court order, Havel obtained DNA samples from Rudner and Foster and sent them off to the University of Nebraska Medical Center's DNA lab. He also obtained search warrants to examine the suspects' homes.

At the young woman's apartment, Havel found a spent 12-gauge shotgun shell, which was identical to the ones retrieved at the murder scene.

At Foster's home, Havel opened a closet and saw a blood-splattered shirt and pants. The closet also held Foster's jacket, which had bloodstains on it. From the pocket, Havel pulled out a spent .410 shotgun shell and a Navy belt buckle — items reported taken in the Iowa burglary. He also discovered a pair of sneakers with the tread and size matching the footprints by the back porch of the Strickland home. In a dresser drawer, he picked up a box of 12-gauge shotgun shells identical to the ones stolen from Kegle and found at the murder scene.

Because the couple refused to talk to Havel about the murders, he waited for the results from the DNA lab. Tests soon confirmed he had tracked down the real killers. The DNA on the pipe matched the DNA of both suspects. Rudner's DNA was on the ring. And Warren Strickland's DNA and blood were on Foster's jacket and sneakers.

Rudner and Foster were arrested on two counts of first-degree murder and two counts of weapons violations in addition to grand auto theft. Although confronted with the overwhelming forensic evidence, Foster refused to talk. However, Rudner finally confessed to Havel.

"We were in a small town in Nebraska and stopped off to eat at a restaurant," she said.

Havel showed her a photo of Husker's Bar and Grill. "Is this where you ate?"

"Yeah. We met a couple of guys — Sam and Luke — I don't know their last names."

Havel pulled out photos of Nichols and Mathews. "Are these the men?"

"Yeah. We shot pool and talked. One of them complained he got fired by his uncle and mentioned his uncle was wealthy. So Gage managed to get the uncle's name, and I looked up the address in the phone book. After we left the two guys, Gage and I decided to rob the uncle and went out to his house."

Havel showed her a photo of the Stricklands' home. "Is this the place?"

"Yeah. Gage waited by the back door while I took off a screen and opened the window and slipped into the kitchen. Then I tiptoed to the door and opened it. Gage had two shotguns and gave me one of them. We intended to use them only to scare the people or to kill any dogs that tried to attack us.

"I found five hundred dollars in an envelope on the kitchen counter and stuffed the money in my pocket. Gage was sure there was more, so we went upstairs. The stairway creaked real loud and woke up the man. He got out of bed and lunged for us, so Gage shot him and I got sprayed with blood. I don't know why, but then I shot him, too.

"The man's wife screamed and grabbed the phone, and Gage blasted her. We panicked and ran out of there and drove straight to Louisiana."

"What did you do with the murder weapons?"

"We tossed them in a ditch during the night somewhere in Kansas."

"Did Luke Mathews and Sam Nichols have anything to do with the murders?"

"No. We did it on our own. They didn't know anything about our plans."

With no physical evidence against Mathews and Nichols, Havel urged the county prosecutor to drop all charges against them. Sheriff Bailey was opposed to it, claiming Mathews had confessed. However, the prosecutor agreed with Havel that the confession was false and given under duress. The men were freed.

Havel stood off to the side in the lobby of the county jail when Mathews walked out wearing street clothes for the first time in seven months. "I'm free!" he yelled, rushing to his parents and hugging them. "It's over! I can come home now."

Havel smiled. He couldn't remember the last time he was glad to see a murder suspect released. But on this day, he was pleased, because it meant he had caught the real killers.

In 2007, Gage Foster pled guilty to two counts of second-degree murder and one count of using a firearm to commit a felony. "I feel sorry every day for what I did," he told the court. "I wish I could take that day back." The judge sentenced Foster to two consecutive life terms in prison. Julia Rudner also pled guilty to two counts of second-degree murder. She told the court, "I'm deeply sorry for all the pain I've caused." Like her boyfriend, Rudner was sentenced to two consecutive life terms in prison.

The Case of the Creepy Cybernapper

The parents didn't have to say a word for FBI agent Kristine Mitchell to know what was racing through their minds. She could read it in their weary eyes, red from sleepless nights and tear-filled days; and in their anguished faces, rippled by unrelenting tension and bouts of fear.

They were wondering when, or if, their missing child would ever be found.

As a member of the Crimes Against Children Task Force, Mitchell had seen this heartbreaking look of despair more times than she cared to remember. She was sitting in the modest Pittsburgh home of Curtis and Annette Kozlowski, gently questioning them about their 13-year-old daughter, Ashley, who had been missing for two days.

The parents handed her a recent photo of their daughter. Studying the willowy teen's high cheekbones, shoulder-length chestnut hair, and blue-green eyes, Mitchell said, "She's so pretty she could be a model."

The 39-year-old agent specialized in hunting down child abusers, kidnappers, and "travelers" — evil men who troll the Internet for kids, befriend them, and travel across state lines to abduct them. On this wintry day in 2002, the agent had been updated by police who brought her in on the case after they had failed to uncover any meaningful clues over the fate of Ashley, who disappeared on the evening of New Year's Day.

"Tell me about the night you last saw Ashley," Mitchell asked the heartsick parents.

"I had fixed a traditional pork and sauerkraut meal for good luck for the new year," Mrs. Kozlowski recalled. "Ashley's older brother and grandparents ate with us, and we all had a good time. About six in the evening, we finished and cleared the table. Ashley said she was going up to her room and would be back down in time to have my apple-walnut pie for dessert. It's her favorite." Mrs. Kozlowski wept and then blurted, "We haven't seen her since."

"Was there a note or any sign she was intending to leave?" asked the agent.

"No," said Mr. Kozlowski. "She just vanished. She didn't even take her jacket — and it was very cold, in the teens."

"Did she take her purse or wallet?"

He shook his head. "There's a pile of cash still sitting on her dresser. There must be at least two hundred dollars in Christmas money."

"Was she having trouble at school or doing drugs?"

"Absolutely not," replied Mrs. Kozlowski. "She makes the honor roll and doesn't complain much about school. She has some friends, although she's shy and reserved."

"Has she ever run away before?"

"Never. She's very cautious and gets easily scared. She's so afraid of the dark that she sleeps with a night-light. When the sun goes down, she turns on every light in the house."

Mr. Kozlowski said, "I searched every square inch of our house, even the cabinets and under the beds, thinking maybe she was playing a trick on us. I looked around our yard and walked up and down the streets of the neighborhood shouting her name. My wife was phoning Ashley's friends, asking if they'd seen her. We got desperate and finally called the police."

Mrs. Kozlowski dabbed her eyes. "The police said she'd probably show up in a few hours. But we knew Ashley was gone." She started to cry again. "I can't eat or sleep. I can't stop picturing her out there, somewhere in the cold and the dark, afraid and in danger."

Mitchell examined Ashley's cluttered second-floor bedroom. The wall was plastered with posters of boy bands, the floor was littered with sweaters and jeans, and her unmade bed held several small teddy bears. The night-light was on, and the Christmas money lay untouched on the dresser. Mitchell poked through the girl's belongings but didn't find any clues. There was no sign of forced entry or any evidence that Ashley had been taken against her will.

Next to the teen's bedroom was a combination family room and office with a computer, scanner, and webcam.

"Does Ashley use the Internet much?" the agent asked, deliberately using the present tense rather than the past tense.

"She uses the computer to e-mail friends and do research for her reports, that's all," replied Mrs. Kozlowski. "Sometimes I'd catch her late at night on the computer, but it was only because she was still doing homework."

Or at least that's what Ashley told her, thought Mitchell. The agent turned on the computer and eyeballed Ashley's SENT and RECEIVED boxes in her e-mails, looking for anything suspicious. She also checked the search engine for bookmarks and recent Web sites that Ashley had visited. The agent clicked on Ashley's personal Web page and noticed the girl called herself "hebejebe" (Hebe was the Greek goddess of youth). Ashley had listed her interests as poetry, modeling, hypnosis, and mythology.

Nothing out of the ordinary, thought Mitchell. *If Ashley is a typical teen, she has told friends secrets she wouldn't share with her parents. I've got to get her friends to open up.*

Later that day, the agent questioned Ashley's small group of friends. It paid off when 14-year-old Savannah Jacobs revealed, "Ashley told me she had made friends with a man in an online chat room. I don't know his name or where he lives. She said she had been communicating with him through instant messaging way into the night."

"How long had she been doing this?"

"About a month. There were a couple of times before Christmas break when she came to school dog-tired because she had been IMing with him until three or four in the morning."

"Can you tell me anything else she said about him, anything at all?"

"No, just that he was in his thirties and was so nice and supportive. She really felt close to him, that he was the only one who truly understood her."

"Did she tell you she planned to meet him in person?"

"No." Savannah shuddered. "I'm so scared for her."

Mitchell returned to Ashley's home and talked again with her parents. When the agent told them what Savannah had said, they were surprised.

"This is the first I've heard of Ashley and this man," Mrs. Kozlowski said. "If Ashley was communicating with him, why didn't you find the messages on the computer?"

"She could have deleted them," Mitchell answered. "But we have ways to find them. You might not realize it, but every keystroke can leave a trail."

Wringing her hands, Mrs. Kozlowski said, "How could she have been communicating with a strange man under our very noses? We trusted her. We thought she was smarter than that."

Mitchell gave her a sympathetic hug and then reached for her cell phone. "I'm going to call in my partner, Todd Pittman. He's an FBI computer specialist. If anyone can find a clue in this computer that could lead us to Ashley, it's Todd."

She walked into another room and called Pittman. "Drop everything and get over here right away," she ordered. "Time is running out. I need you to get inside this machine and find out anything and everything you can about who she's chatted with. This is a life-or-death situation. Every minute counts."

While waiting for Pittman to arrive, Mitchell tried to maintain an air of optimism, masking her fear that the FBI might be too late. She chose not to tell the parents that if Ashley had been abducted by an online predator, her chances for survival were slim. Of those children who were abducted and then murdered, 74 percent of them were killed within three hours of being kidnapped.

"If this man has taken my daughter, he must be a monster," said Mrs. Kozlowski. She began to cry again. "I'm no fool. I know the statistics. It's a one-in-a-million shot that I'll ever see my child again."

"Someone always wins the lottery with worse odds than that," the agent said. "Don't give up hope."

In the living room, Mr. Kozlowski handed photos of Ashley to the Pittsburgh media, appealing for help. Neighbors stopped by, offering comfort and bringing food that would go uneaten. Meanwhile, friends, police, and volunteers continued to search the nearby woods and gullies.

Pittman arrived at the house. The FBI cybersleuth was an expert in the growing field known as computer forensics, which can examine computers and find old Internet searches and even deleted e-mails to help solve crimes. He turned on the family's computer and began copying files and logs, preserving them for a detailed examination at headquarters later.

"Information is stored in an organized manner in a computer, leaving a trail of the user's every action," he explained to Ashley's parents. "Every e-mail and message on the computer is documented, dated, and timed. A computer can sometimes reveal more evidence than a crime scene. A murderer can wipe his fingerprints clean, but he can't easily erase for good what he types on a computer. Even when he has deleted a message, it often still can be found."

Returning to the FBI office, Pittman ran a special software program that examined the hard drive. It yielded tens of thousands of numbers and letters scrambled together. He searched the data for bits of keywords from Ashley's Web page — mythology, hypnosis, poetry, and modeling — hoping to discover other clues amid the jumble of characters. According to the computer's recent activities, Ashley had visited chat rooms dedicated to mythology.

"Kristine," Pittman said, "I think I found something. Ashley had been chatting quite frequently with someone by the screen name **hadesofdc**. Could that be Hades of D.C., as in Washington, D.C.?"

"Could be," she said. "How well do you know Greek mythology?"

"I think Hades was the god of the underworld . . ."

"He was . . . and also the enemy of all life. The guy using that Internet name could be every bit as dangerous as we feared. According to Greek legend, Hades also was a kidnapper. He abducted a goddess named Persephone. This isn't looking good, Todd."

Pittman searched the Internet for references to anyone using that screen name, but nothing surfaced. "Ashley's hard drive isn't giving up any secrets easily," he complained. "The guy must have showed her how to cover her tracks. We need a break."

It came later that night when Mitchell received a phone call from an agent at the FBI office in Tampa, Florida. "Someone called claiming to have information about a missing girl in Pittsburgh," the Florida agent told her. "He refused to leave his name because he was scared, but he agreed to call back. We traced the call to a pay phone. That's all we have at the moment."

"Okay, if he calls back, patch him directly to my line," said Mitchell.

An hour later, the man phoned again and was put in contact with Mitchell, who could tell from his shaky voice he was frightened. "I'm really nervous about all this," he told her. "I want to come forward, but I'm afraid you'll think I'm involved in this kidnapping. I'm not. Honest."

Trying to put him at ease, she said, "I believe you. It's important you reveal what you know about this missing girl. Her life is at stake."

"I've been instant messaging with a guy named Riley. He's from Virginia. We belong to a mythology club on Yahoo. He had mentioned he was looking for a goddess to turn into his slave. The day after New Year's, Riley IMed me, saying, 'I found my Persephone in Pittsburgh.' I IMed him back that I didn't believe him. So to prove he wasn't lying, he posted a webcam image of a girl."

"What did she look like?" Mitchell asked, scribbling down on a legal pad everything he was saying.

"She had long, dark hair. Pretty. Maybe fifteen years old."

"Was she alive?"

"Yeah."

Thank God that fiend hadn't killed her yet, the agent thought. "E-mail me the picture."

"I deleted it, like all the others. Gotta go. I don't want this call traced to me. I'll call you later from another phone."

Click.

He called two hours later and described to Mitchell the photo Riley had e-mailed him: "It was from the waist up. She had kind of a blank look on her face. Her hands were behind her back, so I couldn't tell if she was tied up. But it seemed like the picture was taken in his dungeon. He has sent me pictures of his dungeon before. It has all sorts of chains and shackles. I still had my doubts he had kidnapped a girl. I thought maybe he staged it because he had never sent anything like that to me before. So I went to the Pittsburgh newspaper Web site and found a story about a missing girl. There was a photo of her, and it definitely was the same girl in the picture Riley had sent me."

"What's Riley's Yahoo screen name?"

"I'm not sure . . . **lookingforgoddesses**, maybe. I'm gonna go now. I know your agents are tracing this call, and I don't want to be involved anymore."

"No, wait . . ." Mitchell heard the click.

She hustled over to Pittman and pointed to her notes. "This may be the suspect's screen name. See if he has his own personal profile or Web site."

Pittman searched chat groups and elsewhere on the Internet for anyone using that screen name. But after 90 minutes, he still hadn't found the site.

"I fear this guy is going to kill her soon," Mitchell fretted. "Think of something, Todd."

Pittman snapped his fingers. "Maybe his screen name isn't exactly the way you wrote it down."

Mitchell frowned. "I wrote word-for-word what the caller told me."

"But what if his screen name uses Web shorthand? What if he uses the number four instead of the word *for*? A minute later, he shouted, "Eureka! I've found him."

Mitchell rushed over to Pittman's computer.

"I pulled up a Yahoo chat profile for a suspect using this," said Pittman, pointing to a name on the screen. It read **looking4goddesses**.

Mitchell kissed his forehead. "You're brilliant, Todd!"

"Thank you," he said, not taking his eyes off his computer screen. He glanced at the Web page. "Wow. This definitely is our man. In his profile, he lists other online aliases — including **hadesofdc**."

The Yahoo profile didn't contain a last name, but it did have photos of a dungeonlike basement. One picture showed an overweight, mustachioed man with long, stringy brown hair.

He was posing in front of a wall of bizarre instruments and devices.

"That's the kidnapper," Mitchell declared. "We must get to him before he tortures and kills her."

It was now the third day of Ashley's disappearance. About 7 A.M., the man from Florida called again. "Riley sent me another image," he told the agent. "This time, the girl's arms are bound. And she's crying. Gotta go. Bye."

Mitchell needed to find someone at Yahoo who could provide the Internet Protocol (IP) address of the computer Riley had been using. Like a fingerprint, an IP address is a marker that can identify, with a simple Web search, someone's Internet service provider. From there, the FBI could find the name and address of the kidnapper in the photos.

Mitchell contacted Yahoo at its corporate offices in Sunnyvale, California. At an executive's request, she faxed a letter to Yahoo asking for the IP address. Although that information is usually private, a new law allows Internet companies to reveal names when someone is in immediate danger. If ever there was a case where this applied, it was this one.

By 11 A.M. Pittsburgh time, Yahoo faxed back a 10-digit number, the IP address of Riley's computer. Pittman immediately ran a Web query and discovered Riley's Internet service provider was Verizon. Mitchell called the company in Texas. A Verizon representative gave her the name and address of the customer registered to the account — Riley Walter Tryon of Herndon, Virginia, 240 miles from Pittsburgh.

With Tryon's address confirmed, Mitchell contacted the FBI's Washington, D.C., field office, which dispatched a team of agents to Tryon's home. Now Mitchell, Pittman, and the rest of the Pittsburgh staff only could wait nervously for word of Ashley's fate.

Mitchell phoned the Kozlowskis. "There's been a development," she announced. "We're pretty sure we know who kidnapped your daughter. Have you ever heard of Riley Walter Tryon?"

"No," said Mr. Kozlowski. "What about Ashley? Is she . . ." His voice trailed off.

The agent knew the word Mr. Kozlowski couldn't utter was *dead*. "We don't know anything else at this moment," she said. "I suggest you get down here right away."

The couple arrived at the FBI office 20 minutes later and were led by Mitchell and Pittman to a conference room where a speaker phone was set up on a table.

"We're waiting to hear what our D.C. team found at Riley Tryon's house," the agent explained. "We think he met Ashley in an online chat room and lured her into trusting him. If he's a typical cybernapper, he flattered her. Then he searched for her weak spots — family problems, troubles with classmates — and exploited them. He became her confidant. We call what he did 'grooming.' It's probably been going on for many weeks."

With his elbows on the table, Mr. Kozlowski cupped his head in his hands. Mitchell felt so sorry for him. Judging from his weary face and bloodshot eyes, she figured he hadn't slept since his daughter went missing.

Mitchell couldn't sit down. She was too antsy. *Why haven't the agents called yet? It's been a half hour since they were supposed to raid his house. Did something go wrong? Was it the right address?* Every minute that passed, the tension mounted. *How much longer?*

Ring! Ring! Mitchell practically leaped across the table. She pushed the button on the speaker phone. "Agent Mitchell here." Then she held her breath.

"This is Agent Segura from the D.C. office," said the voice. "We've found the girl. She's alive and safe!"

The room erupted in cheers. Tears welled up in Mitchell's eyes. "Thank God!" There were few things she experienced on the job that made her feel as good as knowing she had helped save a child's life.

"Oh, mercy me!" shouted Mrs. Kozlowski. "She's come back from the dead!"

Mr. Kozlowski didn't move. He just wept out of sheer happiness.

"What happened?" Mitchell asked Segura.

"We went to Tryon's townhouse. No one answered, so we burst through the front door with guns drawn. The house appeared to be empty. But we found Ashley in an upstairs bedroom. She was cowering in the corner, collared and chained to a bolt in the floor. The chain was just long enough to let her use the bathroom."

"What is Ashley's condition?"

"Not bad. She's suffered some cuts and bruises, and she's

pretty shaken up. She's on her way to the hospital for an examination. The good news is she's not seriously injured."

"What about Tryon?"

"He's not there. He had left in the morning, telling Ashley he was going to work. Before leaving, he threatened to kill her if she yelled or tried to escape. She didn't say a word when we broke into the house. She thought he had returned to kill her. We know where he works — a computer consulting firm. We've sent agents to arrest him."

A half hour later, a second FBI team arrested Tryon at a software engineering firm. Ironically, the company's Web page included a link to the National Center for Missing and Exploited Children.

Tryon, a 38-year-old twice-divorced computer expert with no criminal record, didn't resist when he was captured. During FBI questioning, he confessed he had abducted Ashley and planned to use her as his slave. From interviews with the kidnapper and the victim, the FBI pieced together what had happened:

Ashley was shy and didn't fit in well with her classmates. But on the Internet, she could be anyone she wanted. She chose to be a goddess and soon met Tryon in a chat room. She fell under his spell and even though she knew his age, she believed he was her best friend and began confiding in him. If she had an argument with her friends or family, she told him about it, and he always sided with her.

Because he wanted to keep their online relationship secret, he taught Ashley how to "wipe" her computer, eliminating all traces of their communications. On New Year's Day, he arranged to pick her up and drove from Herndon to Pittsburgh. Shortly after 7 P.M., Ashley sneaked out of the house and met Tryon, who was parked a few blocks away. By the time she realized his wicked plans, it was too late to escape. During her captivity, she ate only once and was beaten several times.

The morning after her rescue, the FBI flew Ashley's parents and grandparents to Virginia by private jet for an emotional reunion. Ashley and her family spent about an hour together at the airport before everyone returned home in the jet.

When Mitchell called a few days later to check on Ashley, her mother told the agent, "She's doing great. Everything is back to normal except for one thing. She no longer has access to the Internet."

In March 2003, Tryon pled guilty to two federal charges and was sentenced to 19 years and seven months in federal prison.

Three years after her abduction, Ashley began speaking to student groups about her terrifying experience, warning them about the dangers of the Internet. She became a member of Teenangels, a national online-safety group. "I just want to tell kids: Don't trust anybody online," she has told young audiences. "If you do chat, talk only to people you know from school, people you can actually call on the phone. I was always on the computer. I was addicted to it. I made a lot of mistakes when I was thirteen. [The abduction] nearly destroyed my life and my family. I was almost another body in the morgue."

The
Case of the
Killer Eagle
Scout

At first, there didn't seem to be anything suspicious about the death. Gene Kingston, a 37-year-old eccentric who lived alone, was found dead on the floor of his locked house. His body had been decomposing for several days in the August heat in 2003 when it was discovered by his mother. Because he had health issues and was on medication, authorities initially assumed he died from an illness. However, an autopsy was scheduled to determine the exact cause of death.

Slater Vann, chief of detectives for the sheriff's office, had heard about Kingston while having lunch with a deputy who had been at the scene. The conversation quickly turned to a more pleasant subject — the upcoming football season — when Vann was called to the medical examiner's office.

Ten minutes later, he sat across the desk from Dr. Henry Zito, who had performed the autopsy. "Slater, we have a murder on our hands," he declared. "The body was badly decomposed, but I noticed on close examination there were suspicious marks on his torso. In the autopsy, I found three stab wounds — two through the back and one through the heart — made by a good-sized knife with at least an eight-inch blade."

"So he was stabbed to death."

"Actually, no. When I rolled the body over, I noticed liquefied brain tissue leaking through a hole the size of a quarter in the back of the head. He had been shot to death. Because of the nearly bloodless nature of the knife wounds, he had been stabbed after he was already dead."

"Did you find a bullet?"

"No. He died from a shotgun blast."

"Wouldn't a shotgun blow off his head?"

"Not if the killer used a deer slug. I'm a hunter, and I know that a deer slug is solid enough to drop a buck at fifty yards and yet brittle enough to shatter into shrapnel after entering a skull. If the slug struck the victim's skull just right, it would turn his brain into mush and wouldn't leave an exit wound."

"When did he die?"

"Between six P.M. Saturday night and six A.M. Sunday. I could tell because of the insect activity on the body — especially blowflies." This species of insect feasts and lays its eggs on the exposed dead bodies of humans and animals. Over the years, the blowfly has been studied under carefully controlled environmental conditions. As a result, scientists know, depending on the temperature, just how long it takes blowflies to go from newly deposited eggs to their adult stage. Based on their development, it's possible to determine an approximate time of death.

There were few murders in this quiet Midwest farming county. Most homicides that Vann had investigated involved domestic violence taken to the extreme when one family member killed another. He wondered if this would be another such case.

Vann drove 10 miles from town to the old farmhouse where Kingston had lived. It was now a murder scene, cordoned off in yellow tape. He and other members of the sheriff's office searched every room and the yard for clues.

Like he did in all murder cases, Vann looked for the victim's personal notepads, diaries, and address books. He found an address book that didn't reveal anything. He went through the drawers and saw only a few unpaid bills. Playing back Kingston's answering machine, Vann heard messages only from the victim's parents. Phone records that he obtained days later didn't uncover any suspicious calls in the past month.

Kingston's distressed mother went through the house to see if anything was missing. After offering his condolences, Vann asked her, "How did you discover Gene's body?"

"With his health and emotional problems, we stay in close touch," she replied. "I was in Milwaukee for a wedding, so I didn't see him for several days. I kept calling, but he didn't answer, which wasn't like him. When I returned from Milwaukee, I went straight to his house. The back door was locked. He never locked his door, not even when he left home. His dog, Mandy, was chained outside, barking. There was no water or food in her dishes, which was so unlike Gene because he loved that dog. I had a key and went inside, and there was this awful smell, and then I saw his body . . ." She broke down and sobbed.

After she regained her composure, Vann asked, "Is anything missing?"

"No. His watch and billfold — with money and his credit card — weren't touched. Nothing was taken . . . except . . . I can't find his keys anywhere. He kept them on a key ring on a hook on the wall in the kitchen. He was so precise and tidy."

"Did anyone hold a grudge against him?"

Fighting back the tears, she answered, "He never harmed or angered anyone even though everyone considered him the town oddball."

Hoping to gain a clue by learning more about the victim, Vann said, "Tell me about your son."

"Gene was a sweet, frail boy who didn't have many friends growing up," she replied. "He just never seemed to fit in with the others. He was a good student and earned a college degree. He wanted to be a teacher, but his health and emotional problems prevented him from getting a full-time job. He liked tending to his vegetable garden. He was a vegetarian — and made his dog a vegetarian, too. He was a clean freak. He would take two, sometimes three, showers a day."

She wept again. "Who would kill a lonely, mild-mannered man?"

As Vann started to leave, he looked in a wastebasket by the back door and spotted a balled-up piece of butcher paper with a bloodstain on it. *It's probably from a piece of meat,* he thought. *Wait a second. Gene and his dog were vegetarians. Why would there be meat here? Maybe this bloodstain is from a human.* Carefully, he slipped the paper in a plastic bag so it could be sent to the crime lab for analysis.

Vann and other deputies interviewed people who lived along the quiet rural dead-end road. No one recalled seeing or hearing anything suspicious the night of the murder.

However, Lars Lundgren, the nearest neighbor, who lived a quarter mile away, told the detective, "A few nights before that poor man was killed, an older car came slowly down the road. It had a searchlight on the driver's side, and it was shining a beam on the fire numbers [street addresses] on Gene's house, my house, and the Norquists' at the end of the road. Then the car turned around and slowed down by Gene's house again."

"What kind of vehicle was it?"

"The car sounded old," said Lundgren. "It was a dark color and had square headlights and rectangular taillights."

Vann compared notes with fellow investigator Doug Dahlstrom. "Kingston was a neat freak, yet his bed was unmade, indicating he had gone to sleep and was awakened by the killer," said Vann. "There were no signs of forced entry, so either the victim knew the killer and let him in, or the killer had a key and let himself in, or the killer walked in because the back door was left unlocked."

"The mother said she found the back door locked," said Dahlstrom. "Maybe Kingston was awakened by his barking dog and locked the door out of fear."

"There's no sign he did anything to defend himself," countered Vann. "He didn't grab something he could use as a weapon or call nine-one-one or even attempt to block the door. He apparently had no one to fear."

"So why was he executed?" Dahlstrom asked.

"A better word is slaughtered. What bothers me is the sheer brutality of the crime. He was shot and then, even though he was dead, stabbed three times. A sick and dangerous person did this."

"Why would the killer take the keys?" Dahlstrom asked.

"Perhaps one of the keys unlocks something important to the killer, or maybe the killer took them as a trophy."

Vann ordered his team not to mention to anyone, especially the press, exactly how Kingston was murdered or that the keys were missing. That way, if a suspect confessed, police would know if he or she was telling the truth by revealing facts about the case not known to the general public. Vann had worked cases hampered by mentally troubled suspects who had confessed to crimes they hadn't committed.

Days later, Dahlstrom handed Vann a lab report. "They found something odd," Dahlstrom said. "Under the fingernails of Kingston's three middle fingers on each hand was a mixture of minerals — calcite, marcasite, and dolomite."

"Well, he was a gardener."

"They tested his soil and examined the shoes in his closet. There were no traces of the minerals anywhere. This combination of minerals likely came from only one place — Chadwick Quarry." It was the only quarry within a 50-mile radius.

"Interesting," said Vann. "Kingston was a neat freak who took several showers every day. He shouldn't have had dirty fingernails. Maybe there's a connection between him and the quarry."

Vann visited the quarry and showed workers Kingston's photo. No one recognized the victim or remembered seeing anyone who resembled him at the quarry at any time.

The following day, Dahlstrom told Vann of another finding from the crime lab. "It's definitely cow's blood on the butcher paper you found in the wastebasket," he reported. "They couldn't get any decent fingerprints off the paper. But they did find something else stuck on the paper — a red facial hair either from a beard or a mustache."

"Kingston didn't have a beard, and his hair was brown," said Vann.

"The red hair could have come from the butcher or whoever brought the paper to the house — such as the killer," Dahlstrom said.

Vann went to the grocery store that Kingston frequented but didn't learn anything. However, Max Falcone, the owner of the town's lone butcher shop, told the detective, "The only person I know with a red beard is that high-school star Gary Payne. He was in here last Saturday, right before closing."

"Where have I heard his name before?"

"You know, the 'Big Payne,' two-hundred-fifty-pound linebacker for Anderson High. He's a star on the wrestling and track teams, too. Man, talk about the perfect kid, the one you'd want your sons to be like. Smart, popular, generous. Honors student. Voted on to the prom court. He's the first Eagle Scout we've had in twenty years. Remember? He spearheaded the drive to put up the town's new WELCOME sign. Comes from a good family. Works out at the quarry."

The quarry? Could that be the link between him and Kingston? wondered Vann.

Returning to Chadwick Quarry, Vann learned Gary had just finished his summer job there and was on vacation with his parents before football season started. "I wish I had a dozen Garys," the foreman told the detective. "Nice young man, a hard worker."

Back in his office, Vann called Kingston's parents and asked if they or their son knew Gary. They said no.

Dahlstrom warned Vann, "Slater, I think you're heading in the wrong direction. Of all the people in this town, Gary Payne is one young man who'd be at the very bottom of a list of suspects."

A short while later, a slender coed with short blonde hair was directed to Vann's desk. "My name is Teresa Chadwick," she said. A grim expression clouded her otherwise pretty face. She stared directly at the detective and stunned him when she said, "I think I know who killed Gene Kingston."

Vann sat up in his chair. "Who?"

"My ex-boyfriend, Gary Payne."

"How do you know he killed Kingston?"

"Because Gary told me."

Vann scrunched his face, not sure he was willing to believe her. "I'm listening."

Sensing his doubts, she said, "You probably think I'm an angry girl trying to get even with my ex-boyfriend, but I assure you, Detective Vann, I'm not. I've spent days wrestling in my own mind whether Gary could be a murderer, and now I'm convinced he is."

"Please sit down, Miss Chadwick, and start at the beginning."

"Gary and I met over the summer and began dating. My father owns Chadwick Quarry where Gary worked. I'm a year older than he is and in college. Anyway, we were out one night last week walking along the lake, and we had one of those soul-searching conversations. The discussion got pretty heavy. He asked me to tell him my deepest, darkest secret. So I did. Please don't make me tell you what is, Detective. It's embarrassing, and I swear it isn't criminal or anything like that."

"Don't worry, Miss Chadwick, I won't. Go on with your story."

"Well, after I told my secret, Gary said, 'I have one that's going to blow your mind.' And then he said" — she took a deep breath — "he had murdered that lonely eccentric, Gene Kingston. I didn't believe him, of course. I said, 'You shouldn't joke about a thing like that.' And he said, 'I'm not joking. I shot him in the back of the head and then I stabbed him.' Gary said he took the man's keys as a trophy."

Vann jerked up in his chair when he heard Teresa mention the stabbing and the missing keys. *No one but the killer and whoever he told would know about that,* he thought.

"Did he say why he killed Kingston?"

Teresa shuddered. "That's what's really scary about this. He said he did it just to see if he could get away with it."

The All-American boy killed for the thrill of it? This makes no sense at all. Vann leaned back in his chair and let Teresa's words sink in. He'd been a cop for more than 20 years. Although he served in small towns, he had seen enough of the underbelly of human life, so little surprised him. But this . . . this shocked him.

"Was anyone else involved in the murder?" he asked.

"I don't think so."

"Why did you wait to come forward?" Vann asked.

"Detective, I didn't believe Gary. I'm a pretty good judge of character, and Gary is a warm and thoughtful guy. He does boast a lot. I just figured he had a character flaw about telling outrageous stories. But then I heard you had been out at the quarry asking questions about Gary. And he kept mentioning the murder to me.

"I was creeped out. I asked myself, *Could he really be a killer? And if he is, why am I dating him? He could kill me next.* So I broke up with him. I lied and told him I was heading back to college and couldn't handle a long-distance relationship, but I still wanted to be his friend.

"The thought that Gary is a murderer kept gnawing at me. I couldn't sleep. I couldn't eat. I finally realized I must tell the police. I hope and pray I'm wrong. The only way to know for sure is for you to investigate."

"Miss Chadwick, to get at the truth, to clear Gary of this horrible crime or to put him away because he did it, I need your help."

Later that week, Teresa phoned Gary while Vann listened in on an extension and tape-recorded every word. Her task was to get Gary to talk about the murder. The two chatted about school, and soon she steered the conversation to Gene Kingston.

"Why are you so interested in him all of a sudden?" Gary asked suspiciously. "You always brushed me off whenever I talked about killing him."

"I have to write a scary short story in the style of Edgar Allan Poe in my creative writing class, and I was hoping you could put me in the mood," she lied. "I've got my eyes closed so I can visualize what you're saying. Walk me through the murder."

"Okay," he said eagerly. "It was about one in the morning, and I chose a moonless night so it would be really dark. I parked the car off the road far enough away so no one would see me. I popped the trunk and pulled out a twelve-gauge shotgun and put in a deer slug. I strapped on my hunting knife and put on my gloves. Then I walked to Kingston's house and quietly opened the back door. It was unlocked."

"Wait a minute. Before when you talked about this, you said he had a dog. Wouldn't the dog have been barking?"

"No, because I brought along a bone from the butcher shop and gave it to the mutt. You would have thought I made a friend for life. So I entered the house and crept into the living room, but the floor creaked real loud and he woke up. He walked out of the bedroom and turned on the light. I raised the shotgun and told him, 'Freeze!' He looked like a deer caught in the headlights. I told him to kneel. He did, and then he begged for his life and even clawed at my shoes."

So that's how Kingston got the minerals under his fingernails, Vann told himself. *They came from Gary's work boots.*

"He kept saying, 'Please don't shoot me. Please don't shoot me.' I ordered him to turn around. Then I pressed the muzzle of my shotgun against the back of his head and pulled the trigger. He was dead before his head hit the floor. I turned off the light and pulled out my hunting knife and stabbed him twice in the back. I flipped him over and stabbed him in the heart."

"Why did you do that?"

"For the same reason I shot him. I just wanted to see how it felt."

"How did it feel?"

"It was strange, like it wasn't really me. Like I was watching someone else do this. But then I felt, 'Wow, I just pulled off the perfect murder.' I picked up the shell casing, went into the kitchen, and saw his keys on a hook. I took them as a reminder of a crime that will never be solved. So there, Teresa. Do you have a clear picture in your mind?"

"Vivid and scary."

"Am I not the cleverest person you've ever met?"

Looking at a note the detective had scribbled, she asked Gary, "Who else knows what you did?"

"Just Reed Sorenson. He was with me when I scoped out Kingston's house. About a week before the murder, I told Reed, 'Let's go shining for deer.' So we drove out to that country road, and I was shining my spotlight on the deer, and Reed was getting a big kick out of it. But what I was really doing was getting a better idea of what it was like out there at night. After I killed the guy, I told Reed I was the murderer and showed him the keys, but he didn't believe me."

Reading another note from Vann, Teresa asked Gary, "Why kill Kingston? What did he ever do to you?"

"Nothing. That's why I chose him. There's nothing to link him with me. No connection at all. No motive. That's what's so brilliant about this murder. I picked a victim who lived alone out in the boonies. No one would miss him. He was a loser. I probably did him a favor by putting him out of his misery."

The detective, whose stomach churned from listening to the cold-blooded killer, signaled Teresa to wrap up the call. When she finished, she wept and almost collapsed.

"You did great, Teresa," Vann said. "You should be proud of yourself. Thanks to you, we're going to arrest this teenage monster."

The next day, police went to the high school and led Gary Payne away in handcuffs to face charges of first-degree murder. They searched his house while his parents looked on in a disbelief shared by everyone who knew him. In the basement, police found a 12-gauge shotgun. In Gary's room, Vann discovered a set of keys — later identified as Kingston's — and an eight-inch-long hunting knife in a blood-splattered black sheath. Using DNA samples taken from the sheath, the crime lab proved the droplets came from Kingston's blood.

Gary's car was parked in the driveway. It was a black 1992 Dodge Dynasty — one with square headlights and rectangular taillights, which matched the description given by Kingston's neighbor. Inside the car was a handheld searchlight.

Under questioning by Vann, Gary's friend Reed admitted Gary had told him about the murder and showed him the victim's keys and the bloodstained knife. "The keys could have belonged to anyone, and Gary is a hunter, so naturally there'd be blood on his knife," Reed told the detective. "There was nothing — absolutely nothing — Gary could have said to convince me he killed the guy. I just figured he was putting me on."

When the transcript of the taped phone conversation between Teresa and Gary was printed up, Vann read it carefully. *Life can be so strange sometimes,* thought the detective as he underlined the following passage:

> **Gary**: Guess what, Teresa? I received a letter from St. Cloud University in Minnesota. They said because of my academic record, the fact that I'm an Eagle Scout, and my accomplishments as an athlete, they're offering me a scholarship.
> **Teresa**: That's great. What are you going to study?
> **Gary**: Criminal justice.

Gary Payne pled not guilty by reason of insanity, but a jury convicted him of first-degree murder in 2004. He was sentenced to mandatory life in prison and will be eligible for parole after 32 years. With time served, Payne will be at least 50 before he can even think about getting out of prison.

The Case of the Friday Night Bank Robber

The Friday Night Bank Robber struck again," FBI division chief James Fielding told agent Roy Carlton over the phone. "He hit a bank in Shokan, New York."

Carlton, a 16-year veteran of the bureau, specialized in investigating bank robberies and had helped catch many crooks. But there was one criminal who had outsmarted law-enforcement officials for nearly 30 years — the Friday Night Bank Robber. He was without doubt the most successful stickup artist in U.S. history, suspected of hitting more than 50 banks — all on Fridays — and netting about $2 million.

"It's the same M.O. as his other bank heists," Fielding said, referring to the perp's *modus operandi*, Latin for method of operation.

Carlton knew it well. Just before closing time, the robber would burst through the bank doors and shout in a loud, menacing voice, "Don't look at me!" Even as they recoiled in horror, customers couldn't help but stare at the bandit's bizarre appearance. He wore a full-headed scary Halloween mask tailored to fit so tightly over his face and neck no one could identify his skin color.

Dark, bulky clothes hid his body, and gloves covered his hands. As the terror-stricken people hugged the floor, the robber pointed his gun at them to create the impression that everyone was a potential target.

To prevent witnesses from guessing how tall he was, the thief moved quickly across the floor in a crablike crouch. He vaulted over the counter of the teller windows in a single bound and rifled through the cash drawers, stuffing money in a black bag. Ninety seconds later, he dashed out the door, and with the bag of money slung over his shoulder, he silently vanished into the darkness.

"This time he made off with more than twenty-six thousand dollars," Fielding told Carlton. "It was all so methodical, so careful that police have nothing to go on. He doesn't fit any of the existing psychological profiles. Roy, I want you to work up a new profile of him."

Carlton was an expert in profiling serial criminals — creating a list of physical, behavioral, and mental characteristics about a suspect whose identity isn't known. The typical profile is based on police-gathered evidence, witness accounts, the suspect's conduct during the crime, and psychological guesswork. In

January 2001, Carlton reviewed the case files of dozens of bank robberies in the Northeast that authorities believed were the work of the Friday Night Bank Robber.

"I believe the thief is a loner in his forties or fifties," Carlton told Fielding after completing the profile. "He's a relatively mysterious person who doesn't communicate much with friends or relatives about his personal life. Few people are close to him, and I doubt if anyone knows he's a criminal.

"He's incredibly smart and extremely careful and spends days planning his robberies. The way he handles a gun tells me he's been in the military and is fascinated with weapons, because he's used different ones in his robberies. He wants to scare people, but he won't hurt anyone unless he's forced to. Of all the bank heists he's pulled, only two people have been wounded — both times when an employee tried to be a hero and fight him.

"His signature leap over the counter demonstrates he's in superb physical condition and a fitness fanatic. Judging from the bank-surveillance video, he's about five feet six inches tall.

"All the robberies so far have occurred between October and April when it's dark and passersby are less apt to notice someone wearing gloves and bulky clothing. He strikes about ten minutes before closing because there are fewer people; thus, fewer chances someone will try to stop him."

On April 2, Carlton was in his office when he received a call from Joe Pizzi, a detective with the police department in Radnor Township, Pennsylvania, 90 miles southwest of New York City.

"I came across something yesterday afternoon that we can't figure out," the detective said. "Can you drive over here and give us a hand?"

"What is it?" asked Carlton.

"We found some guns and ammo and other things in a bunker. Two thirteen-year-old boys had been building a fort in the woods yesterday afternoon when they spotted something inside a concrete drainage pipe. They went in and pulled out a foot-long section of PVC pipe that was capped on both ends. The boys were curious, so they opened it and found newspaper clippings about bank robberies and a page of instructions about how to clean a Beretta [a type of handgun].

"The boys brought it here to the police station, and I went back with them to the spot where they found the tube. I soon located a three-by-four-foot bunker lined with bricks and concrete blocks. This wasn't just a hole in the ground. Somebody had taken a lot of time and effort to make it. Inside were dozens of waterproof containers and PVC pipes that held news clippings about bank heists. I also found maps, five guns, five hundred rounds of ammo, food rations, eight Halloween masks, and two ski masks. Everything was organized with military precision. In my thirteen years as a detective, I've never seen anything quite like this. I wonder if it's a cache for some extremist group."

"Did you find any money or lift any fingerprints?" Carlton asked.

"Neither. Whoever used this bunker was very careful."

When the agent arrived at the police station, he stared at the collection of items Pizzi had gathered from the bunker and displayed on a large table. There were seven crudely drawn maps giving the location of unknown sites and photocopies of four topographical maps. Some of the tubes contained handwritten notes on 160 banks in small towns stretching from Connecticut to Virginia. Next to the name of each bank was a letter-number notation such as F-7. To Carlton, F-7 could mean only one thing: On Friday, the bank closed at 7 P.M.

"I'll be," declared Carlton. "I know who this stuff belongs to — the Friday Night Bank Robber!"

He studied the flesh-colored Halloween masks. Some of them were hand-painted with scars and streaks to look more frightening. He examined the weapons — five large-caliber guns, all with their serial numbers filed off so they couldn't be traced. Also in the collection were books on electrical engineering and statistics, a brochure for a karate school, and a tattered and yellowed *Camp Hill Handbook.*

"Have you heard of Camp Hill?" Carlton asked the detective.

"Yeah. It's a prison near Harrisburg. Do you think he's an escaped prisoner?"

"I don't know." The agent thumbed through the handbook. "It looks so old. The copyright says this was printed in 1960. If my profile is correct, the robber would have been a teenager in the sixties. What would he be doing in a prison at such a young age?"

"I just remembered that Camp Hill was a juvenile-detention facility until about thirty years ago," said Pizzi. "He could have spent time there back then, but why would he still have the handbook?"

The agent shrugged. "Maybe he has fond memories of the place," he joked. Then he picked up the karate school brochure and asked, "Ever heard of this place?"

"Yeah, there's a chain of them all over the Philadelphia area," Pizzi replied.

Carlton turned his attention to the seven hand-drawn maps. They had stick drawings of landmarks such as trees, roads, parking lots, and ponds along with arrows and dotted lines and various numbers. "I think these numbers represent the number of paces he walks from a landmark to the site," said Carlton. "The robber is particular and pays attention to detail, yet these maps are crude. He drew the maps this way on purpose to include only enough information to jog his memory. That way, it makes them much more difficult for anyone else to understand."

"What do you suppose they are maps to?"

"Probably other bunkers. What I can't figure out is what the word *Carb* means on the top of each map. Is that an abbreviation for something? Is there a place called Carb?"

The detective's fist hit the table, announcing he knew the answer. "Maybe Carb stands for Carbon County, about seventy miles north of here."

Carlton pulled out his laptop and called up a file containing a list of all the banks the robber was suspected of hitting. "Hmm, this is interesting," said the agent. "He knocked off three banks

98

in that area in the nineties. I better visit the Carbon County Sheriff's Office. Maybe they can figure out these maps."

The agent met detective Fred Quinn, who had been born and raised in the county and was an avid hunter. Quinn studied the maps and concluded the supposed bunkers appeared to be on state-owned land, much of it thick forest. According to one map, one had to walk 225 paces to the north of a remote parking lot, then 155 paces to the east to a boulder. From there, it was another 335 paces to the northwest to the location.

Quinn recognized the area and drove Carlton to a forest preserve. The detective started to count off the paces from the parking lot, but Carlton stopped him. "You're over six feet tall," said the agent. "The suspect is only five feet six. You need to take smaller steps."

Following the map's directions, the two hiked from the parking lot into the forest. After two hours of searching, they found the site — several branches had covered up a neatly dug hole in the side of a small hill. They looked inside, but it was empty.

"This might be a bunker that he plans to use in the future," said Carlton. "Let's put all the branches back and cover it up so he won't know we've been here."

The other hand-drawn maps were harder to figure out and would require days of comparing them to government land maps before anyone could begin another search.

A map marked "Carb-W" had the word *cairn* penciled in next to a turn in a path near a bunker location. Cairn is a word for a pile of rocks used as a marker. The men searched for the cairn for several days before they located it while following a deer trail. Pacing off steps from the cairn, they found the bunker hidden by brush and fallen limbs. Pulling out a three-by-three-foot rock from the opening, they peered inside and saw guns and ammunition cans.

They took photographs of everything in place before touching any of the contents. "It's definitely one of his weapons sites," said Carlton. "Now we know what Carb-W stands for. According to the map, there should be another weapons bunker nearby."

While Carlton began taking an inventory of the guns and ammo inside, Quinn scoured the nearby area. Soon he shouted, "Hey, hey, hey! I've found another bunker!" It was only 20 yards away.

The two sites yielded 30 guns, including automatic weapons, submachine guns, shotguns, and powerful handguns such as Berettas and Glocks. Carlton examined the weapons and noticed the serial number of every one had been filed off. The investigators also recovered about 50 five-gallon buckets containing masks, makeup kits, military gear, climbing gear, ammo, holsters, and magazines. Everything in the bunkers was carried out of the forest for closer examination.

Back at the FBI office, Carlton received some good news from Justin Smothers, a bureau technician. "We were able to read the serial number of one of the guns," Smothers announced. "The stamping process of a gun's serial number actually goes deeper than the surface numbers indicate. Your suspect did a good job of filing off the numbers. But he made one mistake. Like many criminals, he filed the number until he no longer saw it and thought he had removed it. But I ground the metal down past the deepest scrapes to get a strip of polished metal. Then I applied a solution of copper salts and hydrochloric acid, and that made the metal just beneath the stamped number dissolve at a faster rate than the metal around it. I was able to bring up the number long enough to photograph it before it disappeared. I punched the serial number into our database and found it belongs to a pistol that was stolen in 1975 from a shop in Fayetteville, North Carolina.'

"Hmm," said Carlton. "That's where Fort Bragg, the Army base, is located. I wouldn't be surprised if our robber was once stationed there."

Leaving Quinn in charge of finding the remaining bunkers, Carlton followed up on another lead — the karate-school brochure.

He visited several karate schools in the Philadelphia area, asking the owners if anyone matched the profile he had created. He was given several names, and on further investigation all but one were cleared. The lone name that interested Carlton was 56-year-old Chuck Gaylord, an incredibly conditioned third-degree black belt who lived in an apartment within walking distance of the bunker discovered by the two boys.

Carlton obtained a sample of Gaylord's handwriting from the karate school's application form. An FBI analyst confirmed the handwriting matched that of the writing on the maps found in the bunkers.

An examination of Army records revealed Gaylord had received weapons, survival, and self-defense training with the Army Special Forces and had been stationed at Fort Bragg in the mid-1970s — at the very time the recovered pistol had been stolen.

A background check showed Gaylord had a juvenile criminal record for stealing items and then selling them. He spent time in the 1960s in the state's Camp Hill facility for juveniles — which linked him to the handbook found in the first bunker.

Armed with a search warrant, Carlton and police went to Gaylord's apartment, but it was completely empty. The landlord explained Gaylord had moved out on April 2 — the day after the first bunker had been discovered.

"He's very secretive," the landlord told Carlton. "He didn't have any visitors, ever. And he's really weird. He would go running in street clothes with a full backpack. Also, I was in his apartment once to fix a leaky pipe and saw he had very little furniture, just books, a yoga mat, a small table, a couple of chairs, and exercise equipment."

"What did he drive?"

"He had an old beat-up van and car that you'd expect a grandma would drive. He also had a motorbike."

The agent interviewed Gaylord's mother, but she didn't know where he was. She told Carlton her son had received a bachelor's degree in electrical engineering from Villanova University and earned a master's degree in statistics from the University of Pennsylvania. He was a self-employed statistical consultant who earned $7,000 a month as a professional gambler. He was a loner, a fitness nut, and a health-food fanatic who practiced yoga and meditation. He dated many women but never married.

The FBI lost track of Gaylord and, after the 9/11 attacks, the bureau focused most of its manpower on terrorism. Catching the Friday Night Bank Robber was far down on the priority list. Although Carlton's attention was focused elsewhere, he was worried that as fall and winter approached, Gaylord would strike again.

Meanwhile, Quinn kept trying to make sense of the symbols, numbers, and drawings on the maps. He managed to find seven bunkers — some large enough to walk into — carved out of the wilderness. Inside some of them, Quinn discovered more bank-related documents, surveillance notes, clothing, disguises, and survival rations.

In early January 2002, Quinn called Carlton from a cell phone and said, "I discovered a new bunker today. I'm at it right now. It's amazing. The bunker can be seen only by walking past it and then turning around and looking back."

"What's in it?" asked the agent.

"Ammo, survival gear, and masks. It also has some clippings, including one from a magazine about bank robberies. It's dated November–December 2001."

"The fact there's a recent article suggests he might be using this one again," said Carlton. "Don't touch anything. Keep it under surveillance."

On January 28, the agent received a call from Fielding, the FBI's division chief. "Two banks have been hit — one in Harrisburg last Friday and the other in York the previous Friday," Fielding reported. "They look like the work of our elusive Friday Night Bank Robber."

"I had a feeling he would strike again," said Carlton.

As Carlton suspected, Gaylord was spotted returning to the bunker that had been under surveillance. The suspect was then secretly followed to his new apartment.

"It's time to take him down," Carlton said.

Because of the numerous guns recovered from the bunkers and Gaylord's Special-Forces and martial-arts training, he was considered armed and dangerous. So Carlton assembled a SWAT team and tailed Gaylord on the morning of February 7 as the robber left his apartment and drove to Philadelphia. When he parked in front of a library, police swarmed over him. "You're under arrest for bank robbery," Carlton announced.

"You have the wrong man," Gaylord declared.

"Oh, no, I don't. You're the suspect I've been waiting to catch for a long time. And now I've finally got you."

One week before his trial was scheduled to start, Gaylord pled guilty and soon revealed how he pulled off his crimes: He spent countless hours at the library photocopying and memorizing topographical maps, which he used to plan bank surveillance and escape routes. He hit only banks near wooded areas and spent three days and two nights in those woods prior to a robbery, monitoring the routines of the bankers and their customers. Doused in scent-deflecting fragrances to confuse police dogs, he fled with his money into the well-scouted woods for several miles in the dark to a waiting motorbike. Then he rode for another few miles to his van for a clean getaway.

Instead of a possible 115 years in prison, Gaylord was sentenced to only 17 years because he agreed to cooperate with authorities. He led police to 27 other bunkers he had constructed. He taped videos designed to help law enforcers foil future bank robberies. He also turned over $47,000 in cash that he had stolen. Authorities, meanwhile, seized $500,000 from his bank account.

In a one-page letter that he submitted to the court, he said he wasn't proud of what he had done. "While I always rationalized my conduct by believing that robbing banks had no victims, I have come to realize that everyone who was forced to endure the harrowing experience of a robbery suffered tremendous harm, even though they were not physically injured."

— The —
Case of the
Body in
the Barrel

This is going to be a hard case to solve, thought police detective Larry Betton. He had just arrived at a marshy area in the north end of Council Bluffs, Iowa, where the city dumped old trees and limbs. Marked off by yellow evidence flags, a rusty 55-gallon barrel held the skeletal remains of a person who had been partially covered in concrete.

Betton, who only recently had been promoted to chief detective, was in charge of his first big investigation. *I'm going to need a lot of scientific help on this one.*

He walked over to two retired men who had discovered the barrel, which was lying on its side in the weeds. "We were out mushroom hunting," one of the men told him, "when we came across this old steel drum. Parts of it had rusted out, and we wondered what was inside. I gave it a few kicks and made a big hole, and then we saw bones sticking out of the concrete."

"I was a paramedic," said the other man. "I knew immediately they were human remains, so I called the police."

About 75 percent of the body up to the chest had been covered in concrete. Soft tissue like muscles and fat had long since decomposed, so Betton knew the victim had been dead for a long time. However, judging from remaining pieces of clothes — jeans and a blouse — and hair, Betton could tell the victim was a woman.

"Obviously, Larry, she was murdered," said detective Trace Mahorn. "You don't bury a loved one in concrete and encase her in a barrel."

"We have two mysteries to solve," Betton said. "First we have to identify the victim, and then we have to find the person who killed her."

"I know there are a lot of dead trees and brush around here, but isn't it strange no one spotted the barrel until today?" asked Mahorn, who had been on the force for three years.

"Not really," replied Betton, a 20-year veteran who was born and raised in Council Bluffs. "This whole area used to be swampy years ago. But over time, most of it dried up. No doubt the barrel was dumped here at a time when this was all under water. The killer probably thought no one would ever find the body."

On this warm day in May 2006, the investigators combed the marshland on the slim chance they would find a clue that would help them learn more about the victim. They found nothing.

The remains and the barrel, which weighed more than 800 pounds because of the concrete, were carefully transported to the Iowa Crime Lab in Ankeny for extensive analysis.

Days later, Betton received a call from forensic anthropologist Dr. Ken Fong, who had examined the skeletal remains. "The victim was a white woman between the ages of twenty-four and thirty-two years old," said Dr. Fong. "She was about five feet eight inches tall and had short, straight brown hair.

"The victim had extensive dentalwork, including a dental plate on the left side. She suffered a broken jaw on the same side at least two or three years before she died. It could have been from an accident or maybe abuse. Her teeth and bones were otherwise in excellent shape, which indicates she took good care of herself.

"Also, we were able to read a faded number on the tag of her Lee jeans. From that number, we learned from the manufacturer that she was wearing size eleven jeans made in 1983."

"That's twenty-three years ago," said Betton. "Anything else you can tell me?"

"Yes. She was definitely murdered sometime between ten and twenty-three years ago. She had been strangled. We found a piece of wire still wrapped around her throat. The wire was attached to a clothes hanger that had been used as an anchor to tighten the wire around her neck, like a garrote, and strangle her."

"So, we have the remnants of the murder weapon," said the

detective. "That's a good start. Next, we need the name of the victim. Any chance we can get an artist's version of what she looked like when she was alive?"

"Our forensic artist Sally Lindstrom is working on a postmortem interpretation right now," said Dr. Fong. "She should have a drawing ready by the end of the week."

"What about DNA?"

"That's going to be difficult. The victim has been dead a long time. But we're working on it."

In another part of the crime lab, Lindstrom was studying detailed photos of the skull of the victim and going over Dr. Fong's report. Because actual pictures of the body were unsuitable for media distribution, Lindstrom needed to draw an accurate likeness of the victim as she might have been in life. Then her drawing would be made available to TV and newspapers, posted on the Internet, and put on flyers in the hope someone would recognize the victim.

Her long blonde hair tied in a ponytail, Lindstrom stared at the photos of the skull and wondered out loud, "Who are you? Why did you die such a horrible death?"

The photos came from Dr. Fong, who had glued tiny markers at various points on the skull. Each marker (which looked like the eraser on the end of a pencil) had a number that gave the apparent thickness of the soft tissue on the face. The skull was then photographed with these tissue-depth markers and printed in life-size pictures.

Lindstrom placed a piece of transparent paper over the print of the skull and began to draw the victim's facial features.

The tissue-depth markers acted as a guide to the contours of the face. The artist paid careful attention to the facial muscles and the placement and size of the eyes and nose and position of the teeth. Determined to create an accurate likeness of the victim, Lindstrom constantly checked the shape and contours of the skull as well as the measurements.

Soon an image of an attractive woman with rounded cheeks and big eyes took shape. The artist added a facial expression to give the drawing vitality and the look of life. When Lindstrom finished, she eyed the portrait and said, "Everyone deserves a name. We don't know yours yet, but I hope this drawing does you justice and someone recognizes you."

The portrait was given to Betton, who called a press conference. As copies of the drawing were passed out to the media, the detective said, "I appeal to the community to help us identify this woman. This is a drawing of what we think the victim looked like before she was murdered one to two decades ago."

Police weren't prepared for all the phone calls they received. Dozens of people whose loved ones were missing called, believing the remains were those of their mother, their daughter, their sister, their friend. Painstakingly, the investigators checked out every lead and steadily eliminated one missing person after another because dental records or physical characteristics didn't match up with the victim's.

"It's so hard to tell someone that the missing person isn't their loved one," Mahorn told Betton. "They usually cry out of relief, or more often out of frustration."

"Yeah. Every time a family even hears a story like this, it puts a sick feeling in their stomach because they're saying, 'Could this be it?' When a family loses a loved one, they never give up hope. They never give up looking. If they get bad news, at least they can find closure, which can bring a sense of relief."

Eventually, the detectives were able to narrow down the possibilities to one likely woman — Lori Fraser Anderson. The Fraser family said their divorced 28-year-old daughter, who was the mother of a little girl, had been missing since November 1983. Her description fit the physical evidence, and family photos of her closely resembled Lindstrom's drawing, but it still wasn't enough proof. Because of a fire 13 years earlier, dental records that could have helped confirm her identity had been destroyed.

"I need a DNA match," Betton told Dr. Fong.

"We can't get enough usable DNA — the standard form is known as genomic — from the victim's body because the DNA had deteriorated too much over the years," Dr. Fong explained. "However, we have another option. There's a new test that can identify mitochondrial DNA, which we can extract from the victim's bones. This kind of DNA is inherited from the mother, so we need to compare it to a maternal relative."

"That's perfect," said Betton. "Lori had a daughter. She can be tested to see if there's a DNA match. Then we'd know for sure the victim really is Lori."

Lori's daughter, Chelsea, gave investigators a sample of her mitochondrial DNA for analysis, which was done by a crime lab in Minnesota — one of the first times the lab had carried out this new test. It would be several weeks before the results were known.

In the meantime, Betton focused on finding the killer, even though there wasn't much to go on yet. "If it wasn't for the wire and coat hanger found with her, we'd have never known how she was murdered," he told Mahorn.

"Do you think it was somebody she knew?"

"Yes," Betton replied. "The manner of her death — the fact that her clothes weren't torn off — indicates she knew her attacker. The suspect had the ability to get up close from behind and then strangle her."

Later that day, Mahorn, who had sent samples of the concrete in the barrel to an FBI laboratory in Quantico, Virginia, received a report from the agency. "The FBI's analysis showed the concrete was a grade available almost exclusively to construction professionals," he told Betton.

"That makes sense," Betton said. "Our killer probably worked in the business, or knew someone who did. The weight of the barrel with the body and concrete was close to half a ton. That suggests whoever dumped the body either had a lot of help or operated a piece of machinery that lifted it off a truck and into what was then water."

When the DNA results came back, Betton went to Chelsea's home to give her the news in person. Her grandfather, who was Lori's father, was there, too. "It's a match," the detective told them. "Chelsea, the murder victim is definitely your mother . . ." Then, turning to Mr. Fraser, he added, "and your daughter."

Her mouth trembling and her eyes watering, Chelsea said, "I always hoped in the back of my mind that my mother was still alive — that maybe she was struck with amnesia and someday would recover her memory and return to me. Now that slim hope is gone forever." She grabbed her grandfather's hand. "My mother was twenty-eight when she died. That's how old I am now."

Mr. Fraser lowered his head and said, "Detective, this news comes too late for Lori's mother. My wife, Dolores, died last year. She went to her grave without ever knowing the fate of her daughter."

"Who would want to kill Lori?" Betton asked.

Without hesitation, Mr. Fraser answered, "Her ex-husband, Tom Anderson. He married Lori in 1977 against my wishes. I knew he was a no-good bum right from the start. He had a laundry list of run-ins with the law, mostly drunk-driving citations. Tom had a fierce temper and physically abused Lori. One time, he broke her jaw and sent her to the hospital. That did it. She finally got the courage to divorce the brute. The only good to come out of that stormy marriage was Chelsea."

"I was born in 1978," Chelsea told Betton. "Even though I was only three years old when they split, I remember my father beating my mother and sending her to the hospital."

"Did he ever physically abuse you?" asked the detective.

"No, he never touched me. He yelled at me a lot, though. He seemed to take out all his anger on my mother, especially when he drank."

"Had he threatened to kill her after the divorce?"

"Not that I'm aware of," said Chelsea. "My mom and I saw him occasionally after the divorce. She got full custody of me. My dad acted okay sometimes. Other times, he'd argue with her and then storm out."

A wistful smile crept across Mr. Fraser's face as he recalled 1983. "Things were looking up for Lori. That good-for-nothing ex-husband was out of her life. She had a good job as a receptionist in a law firm. She and Chelsea had moved into a new apartment. And she had fallen in love again, this time with a good guy, Mark Dawson, who happened to be Tom's stepbrother. This didn't sit well with Tom. He was enraged."

Chelsea cringed as a painful memory resurfaced. "I'll never forget it," she said. "My mom, Mark, and I were having dinner when my dad barged into our apartment. He was drunk and said, 'There's no way I'm going to put up with my brother living in the same home with my ex-wife and raising my kid.' He and Mark got into a bloody fistfight before my dad staggered out the door."

"Were the police called?" asked Betton.

"No. Mark and my mom thought it only would make matters worse."

"Then what happened?"

"About a month later, Mark took a job in Texas as vice president of sales for an office-equipment company. He said once he got settled there, he would send for us because he wanted us to be with him."

Mr. Fraser picked up the story. "A few months went by, and Lori wasn't sure what to do. It was a big decision, as you can imagine. She planned on deciding by Thanksgiving. On November twelfth, my wife, Dolores, and I were watching Chelsea for the evening while Lori attended a party for one of her coworkers. She left the party at about ten P.M. and was never seen again.

"I checked the hospital and called her friends and coworkers. No one knew what happened to her. Her car was gone. I filed a missing-person's report with the police. They talked to the same people I did, and they even questioned Tom. He claimed she ran off to Texas, but that was poppycock. Even the police didn't believe his story."

"Was Mark investigated?" asked Betton.

"Yes," Mr. Fraser replied. "But he was in Texas the whole time. And what motive would he have to kill Lori? He really loved her. He was crushed by her disappearance. He came to the same conclusion I did — Tom killed her.

"I told police of our suspicions. But there was no evidence of foul play, and without a body they really couldn't investigate further. There was nothing more Dolores and I could do except wait and hope and pray while we raised Chelsea."

"What did Tom do for a living at the time?"

"He worked in road construction — Renker Paving."

"So he had access to heavy equipment?"

"Yes. He knew how to operate machinery — an end loader, bulldozer, steamroller, things like that."

Sounds like he's our man, Betton thought. But he didn't want to jump to conclusions. "Can you think of anyone else who had a reason to kill Lori?"

"None whatsoever," said Mr. Fraser. "She was well liked by everyone."

The detective asked Chelsea, "Do you stay in touch with your father?"

"Rarely," she replied. "He calls me once in a blue moon — usually to ask for money."

"Where can I find him?"

"I don't know. He can never hold down a job. The last I heard from him was about six months ago. He was out of work and living with a friend on the south side of town. Maybe his ex-wives know where he is."

"Ex-wives?"

"Yes. He was married and divorced twice after my mom." Chelsea gave Betton the names and phone numbers of Tom Anderson's former spouses.

Betton interviewed Anderson's second wife, Mary. She told the detective, "Yeah, I was a victim of his abuse. He threatened me more than once, but as you can see, I never disappeared. I was pretty sure Tom had killed Lori. One night, he was drunk and abusive. He told me that if I didn't shape up, I would end up in a barrel just like Lori did. I didn't know what he was talking about at the time, but I could guess."

"Why didn't you go to the authorities?"

"If he killed Lori, then he had little to lose by killing me. I was afraid of him."

Betton visited Anderson's third wife, Shirley, who was married to him for two years. "Oh, he has a temper," she asserted. "In 1997, I filed an order of protection against him after he struck me in the leg and mouth. I had to go to the hospital for stitches."

"Did he ever threaten to kill you?"

"Yes. He told me that if I ever went to the police again, he'd do the same thing to me that he did to Lori — stick me in a barrel of concrete and throw it in the water."

"Is that why you never reported it?"

"Yes. I believe he would kill me if I ever filed charges against him."

"Where is he now?"

"He works as a janitor at the Ballard Avenue Apartments. But promise me you won't tell him I talked to you, okay?"

"I promise."

While Betton was interviewing Anderson's ex-wives, Mahorn visited Renker Paving, which was still in business. Although no one remembered Anderson because so much time had passed since he had worked there, the supervisor confirmed the company back then was using construction-grade concrete similar to what was found in the barrel.

The next day, Betton and Mahorn went to the Ballard Avenue Apartments to quiz Anderson, a burly 52-year-old with thick black hair. They decided not to ask questions that might tip him off that he was their prime suspect. When they flashed their badges, he backed up defensively and said, "Whoa, what's this all about?"

"We're sorry to inform you that we've positively identified the body of your missing ex-wife, Lori, the mother of your daughter," said Betton.

"Gee, that's too bad," Anderson mumbled, his eyes darting between the two detectives.

"We're just tying up some loose ends. When were you divorced from her?"

"I don't remember exactly. The early eighties."

They asked him a series of other simple questions such as "What was the address of the apartment you and Lori lived in?" and "What kind of car did she drive?" With each question, Anderson grew increasingly nervous. His mouth went dry. His hands trembled. Sweat poured down his neck.

"I don't want to answer any more questions without a lawyer."

"Why do you need an attorney?" asked Betton. "These are just routine questions."

"I want an attorney. I've had a few brushes with the law in the past and I don't know where you're going with these questions. I'm done talking to you."

"Well, thank you for your time," said Betton.

When the detectives returned to their car, Mahorn said, "Man, did he have the look of guilt. He might as well have had a neon sign that flashed I DID IT."

They drove straight to the county prosecutor, who listened as they laid out the facts of the case. "We have the motive, the murder weapon, the victim, a link between the killer and the concrete, a history of abuse, and two ex-wives who say he admitted murdering Lori," Betton said.

"Bring him in," ordered the prosecutor.

When Betton and Mahorn returned to the apartment building with several other officers to arrest Anderson, the detectives spotted him on a fire-escape ladder on the fourth floor. He was fixing a vertical pipe that was attached to the wall and extended from the first floor to the roof of the seven-story building.

From the fourth-floor emergency door, Betton stuck his head out and said, "Hey, Tom, we need to talk to you. Would you please step inside."

Anderson panicked. "No way!" He leaped off the fire escape and onto the pipe and started shinnying down.

"Tom, no!" Betton shouted. "The building is surrounded with police. Get back here before you hurt yourself."

It was too late. The pipe broke free from its moorings and bent away from the wall. Anderson held on for a few seconds and then lost his grip. He screamed as he plunged to his death.

Later that day, Betton told Chelsea her father had died in a fall. "There's no doubt your father killed your mother," he said.

"Knowing the truth gives me some comfort, although learning both my parents met violent deaths is hard to accept. I wish it hadn't taken so long for the facts to come out."

"The truth needed all this time to reveal itself," said Betton. "It took twenty-three years for that part of the marsh to dry up so someone could find the barrel with your mother's remains. Had the barrel been discovered a few years earlier, we wouldn't have been able to identify your mother because forensic technology and that special DNA test hadn't been developed yet. Chelsea, remember: Truth almost always wins out in the end."

The county attorney's office declared the case of Lori Fraser Anderson's 1983 murder officially closed. The prosecutor announced he would have had enough evidence to convict Tom Anderson.

The Case of the Bomb-crazed "Grems"

Denver fire investigator Jack Charles was still rubbing the sleep out of his eyes while driving to a crime scene in a residential area. He looked at the clock on the dashboard. *Nothing good happens at 3 A.M.*, he thought. As he rounded a curve, he slammed on his brakes and honked his horn to avoid hitting an oncoming white car that had drifted partway into his lane.

The car jerked back onto its side of the road and rumbled past him. *Probably a drunk,* he thought. He called police dispatch and said, "If a cruiser spots an older model Chevy Impala with tinted windows, stop it and check the driver."

Charles drove three more blocks before pulling into the Bramblebrook apartment complex. Several residents, police officers, and firefighters were gathered in the parking lot around the smoldering wreckage of two vehicles that had been blown up.

Yawning, Charles walked over to the officer in charge, Lieutenant Paul Westfall, and said, "Fill me in."

"About forty-five minutes ago, dispatch received numerous phone calls from residents who reported being awakened by loud explosions," Westfall explained. Pointing to a charred Ford pickup and a Ford Mustang, he added, "Someone turned those vehicles into toast. Fortunately, no one was hurt. My men interviewed the residents, and they all say pretty much the same thing. They heard two explosions and saw flashes of fire."

"Anyone see suspects fleeing the scene?"

"No. I have an officer taking photos of the people lingering around here. You know how some perps love to watch all the commotion they cause."

Charles walked over to the blown-up vehicles, which were parked next to each other, and examined them. Scratching his gray crew cut, the veteran 55-year-old investigator squatted next to the burned remains. From the direction and pattern of the explosions, he could tell one bomb was placed under the front left corner of the Mustang, and the other bomb was put under the passenger side of the pickup truck. He pulled a small notebook out of his coat pocket and wrote, "May 17, 1987." Then he began jotting down his findings.

While searching around the vehicles, he and Westfall found six strands of orange safety fuse (a length of cord filled with combustible material) near the wreckage. He also found a blasting cap (a metal cylinder that connects the fuse with a primary explosive that triggers the bomb). In addition, investigators collected for laboratory processing fragments of duct tape, metal, paper, and foil that likely came from the bombs. Stuck to some pieces of duct tape were strands of dark fiber.

When he finished, Charles walked over to the owners of both vehicles, Ted Trantowski and his wife, Marie, a visibly shaken couple in their late twenties. They were in their robes, clutching each other's arms.

"Do you have any idea who did this?" asked the investigator.

"No," replied Trantowski. "I'm an electrician, and Marie is a second-grade teacher. We've never had problems with our neighbors. For the life of me, I can't think of a single reason why someone would blow up both our vehicles."

"Do you recall any recent arguments with customers or students or parents? Maybe a road-rage incident? Anyone follow you home? See anything suspicious?"

They both shook their heads to all his questions.

The next day, Charles asked dispatch if any police units had stopped a white Chevy. None had. In his mind, there was a possibility the driver could have been involved in the bombings because the car was heading away from the crime scene, although not going fast.

Charles shipped the evidence he and Westfall had collected, including pieces of the vehicles, to the Federal Bureau of Alcohol, Tobacco and Firearms (ATF) laboratory in California. He requested an analysis that could the identity the manufacturer of the fuse and blasting cap and the type of explosive.

The next night, about 2:30 A.M., Charles was once again

awakened by a call from Westfall. "We have another bombing incident. This time a bigger one — a gas station at the corner of Noble and Franklin streets."

Charles yawned. "Can't this bomber strike during normal business hours?"

When he arrived, authorities were examining the Winkles gas station, which was severely damaged by eight explosions shortly after it closed for the night.

"Witnesses basically told the same story as the ones at Bramblebrook," Westfall said. "They heard explosions and saw fire."

Although the bombs weren't big, they caused considerable damage to the station. Separate blasts destroyed five gasoline pumps, two propane tanks, and a small building next to the station. Investigators picked up several expended orange safety fuses that littered the crime scene. Pieces of duct tape recovered from the scene had dark fibers stuck to them as in the previous bombing.

"Well, well, well," said Westfall. "Look what I found." He pointed to an unexploded tube of DuPont Tovex next to the small building. Tovex, a gelled explosive compound intended for underground blasts of mines and quarries, was sealed in a plastic tube that looked like a beige sausage.

"The blasting cap, which would have detonated it, had fallen out of the tube. But the safety fuse is still connected to the blasting cap. It's the same kind of fuse we saw at the apartment complex. I bet the lab reports will show the bombs in both cases involve Tovex," Westfall theorized.

Investigators dusted the unexploded tube and found a set of fingerprints, but they didn't match any known persons. However, the tube did yield a valuable clue. It displayed a ship date code of 85AP2OX. Investigators gave this number to the ATF, which did a records search to determine who purchased Tovex with that code number.

Days later, the ATF told Charles that 99 cases of Tovex with the same ship-date code as the unexploded bomb were sold by the DuPont Chemical Company to the Hyde Powder Company in Arizona. That company, in turn, sold 30 of the cases to the Tellson Mine near Boulder, Colorado, on June 26, 1985.

A week after the latest bombing, Charles and Westfall met with Ray Teller and Dick Layson, owners of the Tellson mineral mine. "The Tovex used in the bombs at the apartment complex and the gas station was traced to your mine," said Westfall.

"That's impossible," Teller declared. "We haven't used any in two years. We keep it locked up in our bunker."

"Who has access to the bunker?" Charles asked.

"Just the two of us," Layson replied. "We have the only keys."

At the investigators' request, the owners showed them the log of all the explosives the mine had used. The four men went into the bunker, where they found the date-ship code of 85AP2OX in 19 sealed cases and one unsealed case containing 50 tubes. But after examining the ledger, Charles said, "Fifty tubes aren't accounted for."

"I don't understand," said Teller. "I certainly haven't used any."

"I haven't, either," said Layson.

"Do you use these orange safety fuses?" asked Charles, pointing to an open box of fuses that looked identical to the ones found at the crime scenes.

"No, we haven't used them for more than a year," replied Layson. He looked in the box and compared it to the ledger. "That's strange. Fifty of them are missing."

Westfall contacted authorities in a 100-mile radius, asking for reports of any bombings over the past two years. When he heard back from them, he was intrigued by a report of a series of fire bombings that occurred a year earlier, in the summer of 1986, when three elementary schools in nearby Westminster were targeted. "The M.O. was different than the one we're dealing with now," he told Charles. "The perps used Molotovs." (A Molotov cocktail is a makeshift bomb made of a breakable container filled with flammable liquid ignited by a fuse or wick that's lighted just before it's hurled.)

"Any leads?"

"Yes. A witness saw three young men in camouflage running away from one of the fire bombings. They hopped into a white car and sped off. Deputies found three different footprints at one of the scenes. All the incidents happened after midnight. There have been no other reports anywhere for more than a year until the recent wave of bombings around here."

"There could be a connection," said Charles. "Your witness mentioned a white car. When I was on my way to the Bramblebrook bombing, I was almost hit by a white Chevy Impala. Go ask the officers who helped investigate the recent bombings here if they recall seeing a suspicious white car."

Two days later, Westfall brought Sherry Mason, a rookie cop, into Charles's office. "Tell him what you saw near the Winkles gas station," Westfall ordered.

The young officer cleared her throat and seemed uneasy. "I drove to a small hill overlooking the station to get a good view of the scene," she said. "I noticed three teenage boys dressed in camouflage. They were sitting on the hood of a white car — an older Chevrolet, I think — and they were watching the action below. I told them it was awfully late and advised them to get home. They got in their car and drove away."

"And you're just telling me this *now*?" growled Charles.

"Sir, I'm sorry. They weren't acting in a suspicious manner. They were just watching . . ."

Charles angrily pounded the table. "Officer Mason, fire setters and bombers often *want* to see the results of their crimes. They *want* to watch the police and firefighters work the scene. Didn't you learn that at the police academy?"

"I uh, um . . ."

"What did they look like?"

"I can't say for certain. They were white, average height and weight. They had on baseball caps, but I could tell they were high-school boys. All three of them were wearing high-top sneakers."

Two months after the gas station bombing, Charles received another late-night call from Westfall. At about 1:15 A.M., a Mustang convertible parked outside a townhouse in a quiet residential neighborhood was destroyed by a bomb placed under the rear of the car. "I'm on my way," Charles said sleepily.

When he arrived, he saw the car had been destroyed by a powerful blast that threw fragments up to 240 feet away. Investigators found pieces of orange safety fuse and duct tape scattered nearby. After examining the wreckage, Charles told Westfall, "It's definitely the work of the same bombers."

The owner of the car was mystified that he had been targeted. "I'm a graduate student in geology," he told Charles. "I'm too young to have made enemies who hate me so much they would blow up my car."

After talking to neighbors, Westfall told Charles, "One witness saw three white males in camouflage running away from the crime scene seconds before the blast. Another resident was riding his bike about a block away when he heard the explosion. He said right afterward a white Chevy nearly hit him as it sped away."

"We've got serial bombers on our hands," said Charles. "Thank goodness, no one has been hurt — yet. It's only a matter of time before there are casualties. We've got to stop them."

The ATF lab results eventually confirmed Tovex was used to blow up the Mustang convertible. The fuse, duct tape, and a piece of the blasting cap all matched the evidence found in the previous two bombings.

"As for the fibers found stuck to the duct tape," the lab technician told Charles, "we did an extensive microscopic examination. They all came from the same source — blue shag carpeting."

Three weeks later, Charles was rousted out of bed by another late-night phone call from Westfall, who told him, "The bombers struck again."

Charles looked at the clock. It was 2:35 A.M. "Don't they ever sleep?" he grumbled. "What did they do this time?"

"They struck Crestview High School."

When Charles arrived at the school, he was met by Westfall and Gil Davis, a senior technician from the gas company.

"At first, I thought it was a natural-gas explosion, but look at this," said Davis, guiding Charles and Westfall to an 18-by-20-inch hole in an outside wall. Coming out of the hole was a damaged three-inch gas pipe that had been connected to the school's emergency generator. "It's not consistent with a natural-gas explosion."

Charles noticed the hole was blown *into* the wall. He also found a section of orange safety fuse eight feet from the blast. "I think the bombers placed Tovex on top of the gas line closest to the building and lit the fuse," Charles said. "They thought that would make a huge explosion, but it didn't, thank goodness."

Unexplainably, the bombing spree stopped as quickly as it had started. Over the next year, there were no similar bombings, although police in the surrounding area investigated reports of pipe bombs blowing up mailboxes, small trees, and garbage cans. Although these incidents didn't seem related to the Tovex bombings, Charles asked law-enforcement agencies to forward to him reports of any bomb or firebomb cases no matter how minor.

One fall day in 1988, Charles learned that a student at Forest Park High had been arrested for possession of illegal explosives.

The student, Sean McCoy, was caught by school officials with several homemade pipe bombs in the trunk of his car.

Charles joined police in questioning Sean, a slightly built teenager who kept taking his glasses off to wipe away tears triggered by his shame and guilt over what he had done. He and a classmate, Elijah Green, confessed to making pipe bombs by following directions from an explosives manual they bought at a used bookstore.

"We thought it was fun blowing up rocks and stuff like that," said Sean. "We made sure no one was around because we didn't want to hurt anyone."

"Do you understand how serious this is, Sean?" Charles asked. "Did it ever occur to you that you and Elijah scared people? That you two could have been injured or killed? That you two destroyed other people's property?"

"I'm . . . so . . . sorry," Sean blubbered. "I promise to pay everyone back for the damage. . . . Please, don't send me to jail."

"Maybe I can help you, Sean. But you have to help me."

"I'll do anything, sir. Anything."

"Sean, do you know who firebombed the schools in Westminster two years ago or bombed the Winkles gas station or Crestview High last year? Any rumors?"

Sean shook his head. "I haven't heard or seen a thing. Honest."

"I believe you, Sean. So here's the deal. Because it's your first offense and you have no previous criminal record, I'll recommend to the judge he put you on probation so you won't do any jail time. In exchange, you'll pay for all damages. And you'll report any information — no matter how insignificant it might seem — of anyone talking or boasting about making bombs or setting fires. Got it?"

"I promise, sir."

Elijah, who was just as sorry as Sean, was given the same deal, which the judge approved.

A few weeks later, Sean phoned Charles and said, "I have some information you might use. At the football game last night, I dropped my glasses down between the bleachers, and I went under the stands to look for them. It was dark. While I was searching for my glasses, two dudes were under the bleachers, but they didn't see me. They talked about blowing up Forest Park High. The first dude said he knew how to do it because he and two other dudes had bombed Crestview and a gas station and some cars last year. He said he could get his hands on explosives because he knew where they were hidden. He said he helped steal them from the mine where his friend's dad worked. I stayed real still because I didn't want them to know I was there. They finally left."

"Do you know who they are?" asked Charles.

"No."

"Did you get a good look at them?"

"No. I didn't have my glasses on and I can't see very far without them. By the time I found my glasses, the dudes were long gone."

"Think hard, Sean. Did any of them mention a name or anything that might give a clue to who they are?"

Sean scrunched his face for several seconds and then snapped his fingers. "Will! That's right. One of them was called Will. I think he goes to my school because he mentioned how much he hated the dean of students, Mr. Fisher."

"Okay, Sean, thanks for your help. Let me know if you hear anything else."

Charles then questioned all eight students at the school whose name or nickname was Will, Willy, Bill, Billy, or William. One of them, Will Trueblood, reluctantly admitted he had talked with fellow student Frank Phillips about blowing up the school. "I wouldn't really do it," said Will. "I was ticked off at the dean because he caught me smoking. Frank said he knew how to set up explosives and could get his hands on some. Please, don't tell Frank what I just told you. He has a short fuse."

My guess is he has many fuses, Charles thought.

When Charles questioned Frank, the student denied he and Will had discussed bombing the school or knew anything about the previous year's bombings. He also claimed he didn't know anyone whose father worked in a mine.

Charles returned to the Tellson Mine and talked with co-owner Ray Teller. "Do you know a young man named Frank Phillips?" Charles asked.

"Of course. He's a friend of my son, Grady. They've been buddies since grade school. In fact, Grady sold his car to Frank last year."

"Oh? What kind of car?"

"A 1980 Chevy Impala."

"White?"

"Yes, how did you know?"

"Lucky guess. Do Grady and Frank pal around with anyone else?"

"They were very tight with Jeremy English, but he moved to Westminster in 1986. Still, the three of them spent a lot of time together over the summer of 1987 when Grady graduated. He's a year older than the other two."

"Where can I find Grady?"

"He's in Norfolk, Virginia. He joined the Navy right after high school." Teller frowned and said, "Hey, you're not suggesting these boys had anything to do with the bombings, are you?"

"Let's say they are people of interest who could help solve this case."

The next day, Charles returned to the school and talked to Frank. "Why didn't you tell me you knew Grady Teller?"

"I'm not a squealer."

"Oh? Do you have something to hide?"

"I'm not talking to you anymore." Frank folded his arms.

"Is that your white Chevy Impala out in the parking lot?"

"Yeah, what about it?"

Charles pulled out a document. "This is a warrant to search your car."

Minutes later, the investigator opened the trunk and saw it was fitted with a large piece of dark blue shag carpet. *So that's where the fibers on the duct tape came from*, he thought. A lab technician later confirmed the carpet was made from fibers identical to the ones found stuck to pieces of duct tape recovered from the bombing scenes.

Meanwhile, Jeremy was brought in for questioning. It didn't take long before he confessed that he, Frank, and Grady had been responsible for all the bombings. Jeremy and Frank, who had no criminal records, were arrested. Only then did police discover the fingerprints on the unexploded tube of Tovex at the gas station bombing belonged to Jeremy.

Days later, the Navy turned Grady over to Colorado authorities, but he remained defiant.

However, Frank and Jeremy told investigators everything. They said as kids, the three played war games and pretended to be superheroes. Later in their teens, they often went camping near the Tellson Mine. In the summer of 1986, they wanted to experiment with explosives. Grady secretly took his father's key and made a duplicate. Then the three sneaked into the bunker and stole about 50 explosives along with 50 blasting caps and fuses. They hid the explosives in a cave near the mine. At first, the teens blew up rocks and anthills, but then they turned to vandalism. Near the end of that summer, the threesome went joyriding in Grady's car and firebombed three elementary schools in Westminster.

The trio began calling themselves "Grems" after a popular movie at the time, *Gremlins*, which was about a bunch of mischievous, dangerous critters that terrorize a town. When the three teens carried out their "missions of destruction," they wore camouflage gear and sneakers. The following summer, in 1987, they resumed their destructive ways by bombing the three vehicles, service station, and high school. The bombings stopped when Grady joined the Navy.

Charles thanked Frank and Jeremy for their cooperation and told them, "I hope you'll turn your lives around."

"I'd planned to go into mining after high school," Jeremy said. "But now I don't want anything to do with explosives ever again."

The Grems pled guilty to the bombings, expecting to receive light sentences because they hadn't caused any casualties. But the judge said their actions threatened the safety of innocent people. Jeremy, the youngest, was tried as a juvenile and received the maximum term for his age — 18 months in a juvenile-detention facility plus five years probation. Frank was given an eight-year prison sentence, but because he was a model inmate, he was released in four years. Grady, who remained uncooperative throughout the investigation and became verbally abusive toward the judge, was sentenced to 18 years in a medium-security prison. All three also had to pay for the damages they caused.

The
Case of the
Missing Pizza-
Delivery Girl

Sheriff's detective Mickey Greco took a bite from a half-eaten cold muffuletta sandwich and shoved a few stale fries into his mouth. He had been trying to scarf down the meal at his desk for more than three hours, but he kept getting interrupted.

"I thought it'd be a quiet night," he told his partner, Darrell Perret.

Greco was wrong. Ever since he came on his shift, he had been unusually busy for a Thursday night in Louisiana's Lafayette parish. First, there was the break-in at a toy store and then a home invasion.

Greco, who grew up in the bayous near here, always wanted to be a cop. After earning his degree in criminology at Louisiana State University, he became a sheriff's deputy and at age 26 became the force's youngest detective. A husky man with dark brown eyes and curly brown hair, Greco loved to eat, especially his all-time favorite, the muffuletta — a round loaf of Italian bread, split and filled with layers of sliced provolone, salami, ham, and olive salad.

About 1:30 A.M. on that sultry September night in 2001, Greco and Perret finished their paperwork and walked toward Nick's Café for a slice of banana cream pie. On their way, Armen Latchey stepped out the front door of Armen's Pizza and hailed them. Latchey was one of Greco's success stories — a petty thief who, with the detective's help, had turned his life around and now owned a takeout pizza business.

"Hey, Armen, how you doing?" Greco said.

"I'm worried, Detective. One of my delivery girls, Brandi Foxx, went on a call and never came back. That's not like her."

"How long has she been missing?"

"About two hours. I tried calling her on her cell phone, but she doesn't answer. I think something bad has happened to her. She's really a responsible young woman."

Greco turned to Perret and said, "I guess the banana cream pie will wait."

The two detectives entered Armen's and gathered some basic information from Latchey. At about 11:20 P.M., a man named Stewart placed an order for a large cheese-and-sausage pizza to be delivered to 598 Augusta Road. About 20 minutes later, Latchey called Stewart to tell him the pizza was on its way.

Brandi put the pizza in her car — a 1994 red Honda Civic with an ARMEN'S PIZZA sign on the roof — and headed for

Augusta Road. She hadn't been heard from since. Latchey called her number and also Stewart's but got no answer. He left a message on both their voice mails to call him as soon as possible. Neither had returned the call.

"Brandi is a spunky, good girl, Detective," said Latchey. "She works three part-time jobs — nurse's aide, hotel maid, and pizza-delivery girl — to help support her disabled mother. Very responsible. She's nineteen. Long brown hair, green eyes, about five feet five, one hundred forty pounds. She had on a red Armen's T-shirt, black shorts, and a red baseball cap. I'm worried about her."

The detectives drove to 598 Augusta Road on the outskirts of town, arriving about 2 A.M. The address was a small farm that included a modest frame house in the front, two outbuildings and a barn on the side, and a small cement block house about 200 yards in the rear. No lights were on. A pickup truck was parked in the back.

Using flashlights, the detectives scanned the driveway and quickly found a pack of Marlboros with several cigarettes strewn nearby. They also spotted a cell phone with its battery detached lying on the edge of the unkempt, weedy lawn that was more dirt than grass. "Looks like a struggle took place here," said Greco, pointing to the scuff marks and dirt on the driveway next to the cigarettes and phone. "I wonder if it's Brandi's phone."

Putting on rubber gloves, Perret picked up the phone and slipped in the battery. The display screen lit up, revealing the phone number. "It's not Brandi's," he said. "But it's the same number that called in the order."

At the end of the driveway, Greco noticed fresh, muddy tire tracks. "Look here, Darrell," he told Perret. "Someone drove out beyond the driveway between the two houses and then turned around and drove back onto the driveway."

"Yeah, those tire tracks left behind a lot of fresh mud. And they're too skinny to match the tires of the pickup."

"I don't like this, Darrell. I'm starting to think the girl is in grave danger. We need to move fast on this one. Let's try to wake up someone."

They knocked on the doors of the main home, the outbuildings, and the house in the back, but there was no answer. Meanwhile, Greco issued an alert for police in the area to be on the lookout for Brandi's car.

About a half hour later, he received a call from Deputy Keith Yulee, who had been searching the area. "Mickey, I found the pizza sign off to the side on Cutter Road, about a mile from your location."

"We'll be right there."

When the detectives arrived, the sign was lying on its side in a field about 20 feet from the road. "We'll get it dusted for fingerprints," said Greco. "It's likely that someone knocked it off Brandi's car . . ."

"Or it fell off while she was racing away, maybe from an assailant," added Perret.

They examined the area briefly with their flashlights but

failed to find anything, so they decided to wait until daybreak to conduct a more thorough search of the field.

Later that morning, while police looked for clues in the field, the detectives returned to 598 Augusta Road. They knocked on the door of the main house, which was answered by a man in his sixties.

"We're looking into the disappearance of a pizza-delivery girl," said Greco. "Her last-known stop was at this address."

"I doubt it," said the man, who identified himself as Eddie Stewart. "I'm the only one who lives in this house and I sure didn't order a pizza. I doubt Mario Mendez did either because he doesn't speak English and doesn't have a phone."

"Who's Mario Mendez?"

"A farm worker who does odd jobs for me. I let him live rent-free in the little house at the rear of my property."

Greco held up the cell phone he found in the driveway. "Does this belong to you?"

"No," said Stewart, pulling out his own cell phone. "Here's mine."

"Do you smoke, Mr. Stewart?"

"No, but Mario does."

"Where were you last night between eleven and two?"

"At the oil refinery. I work the night shift as a supervisor."

"Where can we find Mario?"

"Try the little house out back."

The trio found Mario behind the house, sharpening a machete. A look of terror spread across his face when he saw the detectives.

"We'd like to ask you a few questions," said Greco, who had Stewart act as a translator. "Did you or someone you know order a pizza to be delivered here last night?"

"*No, señor,*" Mendez replied uneasily.

"Did you see a pizza-delivery car arrive here?"

"*No, señor.*"

"Where were you last night between the hours of eleven and two?"

"Here, asleep."

"Didn't you hear us knocking on the door?"

He shook his head. "I'm a very sound sleeper."

The detectives looked at each other and thought the same thing: *He's lying.*

Mendez nervously grabbed a pack of Marlboros out of his shirt pocket and, with a trembling hand, lit a cigarette.

"Mind if we look inside?" Greco asked Stewart.

Tears welled up in Mendez's eyes. He dropped to his knees and clasped his hands in prayer. "Please, don't arrest me. I don't want to go back to Mexico. I'm so sorry I took her. She was all alone by the side of the road, so I grabbed her and hid her. Forgive me!"

While Perret kept an eye on Mendez, Greco charged into the little house, convinced Brandi was inside. He skidded to a stop in the living room and shouted, "What in the world . . . ?"

Standing in front of him was a five-foot-tall wooden mermaid. Greco ran into the kitchen and then into the two bedrooms. He was startled to find a bearded man with a shaved head sleeping on a cot. "Police! Don't move!"

The man, whose face was bruised and had a cut over his left eye, looked up at him and groggily said, "Hey, man, I'm not going anywhere."

"Where's Brandi?"

"I don't know who you're talking about."

"Get out of bed and come with me."

Greco hustled him out and then confronted Mendez. "Where's Brandi? Where is she?"

Mendez walked into the living room and pointed to the mermaid. In frustration, Greco turned to Stewart and said, "What is going on?"

Stewart questioned Mendez in Spanish and then explained to the detectives, "Mario found the mermaid in the parking lot of the Come-Inn Bar. She must have fallen out of someone's truck. He thought she was beautiful, so he took her. He thinks you're here to arrest him for stealing her, which is why he was afraid to answer the door last night."

Greco kicked the front step out of frustration. "I'm not interested in a mermaid. I'm interested in Brandi."

Turning to the other man, Greco said, "Who are you?"

"I'm Lenny Stewart, Eddie's son."

"Lenny, what are you doing here?" asked his father.

"Sorry, Dad. I was out late with Billy and I had a little too much to drink. So he dropped me here to sleep it off."

Eddie explained to the detectives, "Lenny sometimes sleeps over in the little house and even keeps some of his work clothes here as well. He works for the gas company."

"What happened to your head, Lenny?" asked Perret.

"I, uh, fell down. I was drunk."

"Did you order a pizza last night?"

"Yeah."

"Was it delivered here?"

"Yeah."

"Who brought it to you?"

"Some chick. I paid her, gave her a nice tip, and she drove off."

Greco held up the cell phone he had found on the driveway hours earlier. "Lenny, is this yours?"

"Yeah. I wondered where it was. It must have slipped out of my pocket when I fell down."

"Lose anything else when you fell?"

"My Marlboros. Did you find them, too?"

"Yeah. But we're going to keep them and the phone for a little bit."

"About what time did you fall down and hurt yourself, Lenny?" asked Perret.

"Real late, maybe three or four in the morning."

"That's strange, because we found the phone and cigarettes in the driveway at about two."

"Oh, I'm a little confused," Lenny mumbled. "Like I said, I was drunk."

During their search in the little house, the detectives entered the bedroom where Lenny had been sleeping. Greco stared at the bed. *Something isn't right,* he thought. He lifted up the mattress and said, "This is an odd place to keep clothes." Tucked between the mattress and the box spring were a short-sleeved light blue shirt with blood splatters on it and jeans with streaks of charcoal. The detective had a sickening feeling in his stomach — the one he often got when he suspected a missing person might be dead.

"Lenny, why are your clothes under your mattress?" Greco asked him. "Looks like blood and ash on them. And they smell of gasoline."

"I, uh, was helping my friend Billy Delaney burn some trash," he replied. "And that blood is mine. I cut myself when I fell."

Greco stepped within inches of Lenny's face and snarled, "I don't believe you. Now, Lenny, I'm asking you again: Where is Brandi?"

Lenny, who was as big as Greco, glared at the detective. "I told you. She delivered my pizza and drove off. I never saw her again."

Perret's cell phone rang. "What?" he said to the caller. "Where?" When he ended the call, he told Greco, "Deputy Yulee found an abandoned red Honda Civic about five miles from here in a sugarcane field off Cutter Road. The interior had been set on fire. The license plate was burned, but they confirmed it's Brandi's car."

"Was her body inside?" asked Greco.

"No. They're searching the area now."

Greco wheeled around and was nose to nose with Lenny. "What did you do with Brandi?"

"Nothing!" snapped Lenny.

"Time is of the essence. Maybe you'll be more willing to talk to us at the sheriff's office." Without taking his eyes off Lenny, Greco read him his rights.

Turning to his father, Lenny asked, "Dad, do you know a good lawyer?"

Lenny was handcuffed and whisked to the sheriff's office, where he steadfastly refused to answer any more questions. Meanwhile, Greco, who had carefully sealed the bloody clothes into an evidence bag, turned them over to Anna Puffer, a crime-scene technician, for analysis.

The next day, she called Greco and said, "I've found some disturbing things. Inside Lenny Stewart's jeans were several strands of long brown hair. Some even have the roots on them, which implies they were pulled out of the person's head. Obviously, they're not Lenny Stewart's because he's bald. We definitely can extract DNA from them. We're getting a sample of Brandi's hair from her hairbrush at home, so we can compare the DNA.

"Also, I found other things on his pants, such as traces of sugarcane and gasoline. As for his shirt, the stains came from O-positive blood. He has A-negative, and Brandi's mother said she's O-positive."

"She's either dead or kidnapped," said Greco. "And he's not talking. Time is running out."

Days later, the DNA results were back. The DNA from the strands of hair found in Lenny Stewart's pocket matched the DNA in the hair on Brandi's hairbrush.

A thorough search of the field where the car had been set on fire turned up no new clues. However, there was enough tread on the back tires to compare it with the muddy tire tracks at the end of Eddie Stewart's driveway. They were a match.

Greco and Perret visited the suspect's friend Billy Delaney. Delaney claimed he was burning trash at his house with Lenny's help and then dropped Lenny off at the Stewart farm about 10:30 P.M. But when the detectives examined the burned pile, they could tell the ashes were weeks old. Challenged by the lawmen, Delaney admitted Lenny had persuaded him to make up the story.

"You could spend time in jail for lying to us and obstructing justice," Greco told Delaney. "This is your last chance, Billy. Tell us the truth."

"Okay, okay," said Delaney, sighing. "Lenny showed up at my house about three in the morning. He said he got into a bar fight and asked me to drive him to the farm. He smelled of smoke and gasoline. He said if anyone asked, I should say he was with me burning trash. I asked what this was all about, and he said, 'The less you know, the better.' So I took him to the farm and left. I swear to you, that's the truth."

Back at the jail, Greco again questioned Lenny, but the suspect continued to stonewall him. "I have nothing to say to you," he hissed.

"Well, I have plenty to say to you, Lenny. We're charging you with first-degree murder in the death of Brandi Foxx."

"You have no body and you have no proof she's dead," Lenny countered. "She probably ran away or ran off with someone after delivering my pizza."

"We have enough evidence to convict you. You're the last-known person to see her alive. There were signs of a struggle in your driveway. We found Brandi's blood and hair on your clothes. We found the ARMEN'S PIZZA sign from her car, and it had your fingerprints on it. Your alibi has been shot to pieces by your friend Billy. Brandi's car was burned up in a sugarcane field, and we found traces of gasoline and sugarcane on your pants. Gee, Lenny, you think we don't have a strong case against you?"

Lenny shrugged. "Go ahead. Prove it."

Three weeks later, Greco was at his desk eating a muffuletta when he received a call from Deputy Yulee. "I'm in a cane field near Milton," Yulee said. "A farm worker found a decomposed body in a shallow grave. Mickey, I'm pretty sure it's Brandi."

Greco shoved his sandwich aside and kicked his desk in anger. Although he would need confirmation from the police lab, he knew in his heart that it was her.

The official word came from Anna Puffer days later. "The remains are those of Brandi," she told the detective. "We have DNA and dental confirmation."

"How long had she been dead?"

"We can tell from the condition of the body and bones and insect activity that she died around the day she was reported missing."

Greco returned to the jail and once again questioned the suspect. "We found Brandi's remains, Lenny. Now we have a body to go with all the evidence against you. It's time for you to come clean."

The prisoner rubbed his jaw, lost in thought. His eyes began to water. After a minute of silence, he took a deep breath. "Yeah, I killed her," he confessed. "But I didn't mean to do it. I had been drinking at the Come-Inn Bar and I got a lift from a friend to the farm where my truck was parked. I was hungry so I ordered a pizza. When the delivery girl came, I realized I was short five bucks. I didn't have my checkbook or credit card with me — they were back in my apartment in town — so I said, 'Well, give me half the pizza.' I grabbed for it, and she stepped back and fell down, and the pizza spilled out. She got up and called me a jerk, and I slugged her. She socked me in the forehead. I grabbed her by the hair and hit her again, and she fell back and struck her head hard on the driveway. I thought I had knocked her out, so I put her in her car and drove out back, because I was afraid the neighbors across the street would see us. I tried to revive her, but she wouldn't wake up. Then I listened to her heart. She was dead." He closed his eyes and lowered his head.

"What happened next?" asked Greco.

"I panicked. I knew I had to get rid of the body and the car. So I took a gas can and shovel out of my truck and put it in her car. I drove her in her car and went out to Cutter Road. I suddenly remembered she had an ARMEN'S PIZZA sign on top, so I knocked it off the roof and threw it in the field. I went to a sugarcane field in Milton and buried her. Then I drove the car to another cane field and set it on fire.

"From there I walked over to Billy's house. I told him I got in a bar fight and needed a ride back to the farm. Billy drove me there at about four A.M. I had planned on burning my clothes in the morning and putting on my work uniform. But then you guys showed up."

He gazed at Greco and gave a glimmer of a smile. "It feels good to get this off my chest. I'm real sorry for what I've done. I didn't mean for it to end this way."

A look of disgust darkened Greco's face. "Well, here's how I mean for this to end: You'll never be a free man again."

Lenny Stewart pled guilty to first-degree murder in 2004 and was sentenced to life in prison without the possibility of parole, probation, or suspension of his sentence.

About the Author

Allan Zullo is the author of nearly 90 nonfiction books on subjects ranging from sports and the supernatural to history and animals.

He has written the best-selling *Haunted Kids* series, published by Scholastic, which are filled with chilling stories based on, or inspired by, documented cases from the files of ghost hunters. Allan also has introduced Scholastic readers to the *Ten True Tales* series, about kids who have met the challenges of dangerous, sometimes life-threatening, situations. In addition, he has authored two books about the real-life experiences of kids during the Holocaust — *Survivors: True Stories of Children in the Holocaust* and *Heroes of the Holocaust: True Stories of Rescues by Teens.*

Allan, the grandfather of two boys and the father of two grown daughters, lives with his wife Kathryn on the side of a mountain near Asheville, North Carolina. To learn more about the author, visit his web site at www.allanzullo.com.